Developing Your Portfolio
Enhancing Your Learning
and Showing Your Stuff

Portfolios are not just for documenting the work of young children—they can also be powerful resources for early childhood educators' professional preparation and development, from evaluating one's classroom practice to showcasing skills and accomplishments. Veteran teacher educators Marianne Jones and Marilyn Shelton provide practical and comprehensive guidance on developing a portfolio specific to the needs of pre- and in-service teachers of young children. This updated new edition features:

- A flexible and friendly approach that guides students at varying levels of experience through the portfolio process.
- New material on portfolio planning and organization and additional coverage on writing rationales and captions.
- A companion website with additional instructor and student resources such as PowerPoint slides, flashcards, activities, and printable templates for improving portfolio skills.

Both theoretical and practical, this valuable resource addresses issues and mechanics related to process and product, instruction and guidance techniques, the role of reflection, and assessment strategies. With concrete examples, rubrics, tips, and exercises, this book provides a step-by-step guide to creating a professional teaching portfolio.

Marianne Jones is Professor of Child Development and Chair of the Child, Family, and Consumer Science Department, California State University, Fresno.

Marilyn Shelton is Professor of Literacy and Early Education, California State University, Fresno.

Developing Your Portfolio

Enhancing Your Learning and Showing Your Stuff

A Guide for the Early Childhood Student or Professional

Second Edition

MARIANNE JONES AND MARILYN SHELTON

Routledge
Taylor & Francis Group

NEW YORK AND LONDON

First edition published 2006
by Routledge
270 Madison Avenue, New York, NY 10016

This edition published 2011
by Routledge
270 Madison Avenue, New York, NY 10016

Simultaneously published in the UK
by Routledge
2 Park Square, Milton Park, Abingdon, Oxon OX14 4RN

Routledge is an imprint of the Taylor & Francis Group, an informa business

Library of Congress Cataloging in Publication Data
  Jones, Marianne E.
  Developing your portfolio: enhancing your learning and showing your
  stuff: a guide for the early childhood student or professional / Marianne Jones
  and Marilyn Shelton.—2nd ed.
     p. cm.
  1. Portfolios in education. 2. Early childhood teachers—Training of.
  I. Shelton, Marilyn R. II. Title.
  LB1029.P67j66 2011
  372.21—dc22

ISBN 13: 978–0–415–80051–8 (hbk)
ISBN 13: 978–0–415–80052–5 (pbk)
ISBN 13: 978–0–203–83503–6 (ebk)

Typeset in Minion by Swales & Willis Ltd, Exeter, Devon
Printed and bound in the United States of America on acid-free paper
by Walsworth Publishing Company, Marceline, MO

Contents

Acknowledgments

We still feel deeply indebted to the wonderful people who offered information, assistance, and who helped shape our thinking in the first edition. At this point, we would like to thank the many students and faculty who have used our book, given feedback, and asked thought provoking questions. We continue to learn from them. We appreciate our editor, Heather Jarrow, who has been patient, prompt in her feedback, and has provided guidance and resources that have led to the development of the new website. One final thank you goes to our colleagues who participated in the blind review of the first edition and whose written critiques provided us with useful direction for the second edition.

Introduction

You know those days when you realize that things are a little out of whack? You scratch your head and wonder what, exactly, is wrong. The disconnect between how early childhood professionals are taught to address children's learning and how adult learning is approached was, for us, one of those head-scratching things. Constructivist practice—hands-on, interactive, social, collaborative—is so engaging. It made us wonder why it is not happening more in classrooms with adult learners. We wanted it to happen more often in our own classrooms. We raised questions for ourselves such as: "How does being prescriptive with students (the paper must be eight pages long; no longer, no shorter) contribute to their critical examination of a topic?" "How can paper-and-pencil tests help students construct knowledge or learn to be self-evaluative or reflective?" We looked again to some of our Constructivist beliefs: Adults can construct their own knowledge; they will assume responsibility for their learning if it has meaning to them; and, when given a choice and properly scaffolded, adults prefer active rather than passive learning. If these things are true, as we believe, then we had to structure our classrooms—both the cognitive and emotional aspects—to promote them. We moved increasingly from teacher-directed to student-directed learning. We found that using portfolios with students helped us to do this. Portfolios represent an expression of Constructivist learning. They provide an authentic representation of the student's work, learning, and accomplishments.

We've used portfolios with adult learners in child development and early childhood education classes at the community college, baccalaureate, and postbaccalaureate levels over the past 16 years. What we've learned is that it is not easy for students to go from being told how and what to learn to figuring it out for themselves. Over the years we have devised strategies and instruction to help students understand and manage the portfolio process, and keep their sanity. In the process, our guidance and instruction has evolved, and so have we. As we have engaged students in the portfolio process, we have indeed engaged each other in becoming more reflective educators.

In the course of our work, we have read volumes on portfolios, and we have noticed two things. The first is that none of them really address educators across the full spectrum of early care and education—birth through third grade. The second is that none really connect and explain the Constructivist underpinnings of portfolios. This book does both.

This book is both theoretical and practical. We have written it for early care and education students and practitioners: Those who are in community college and four-year university child development or early childhood education programs or courses, elementary education teacher preparation programs, graduate certificate or Master's programs, or working professionals in the field.

What's New in the Second Edition

The basis of the book is the same as the first. We are still committed to our Constructivist way of working with the adults that we teach, of modeling what we preach. The second edition is updated with new content on planning, organizing, and writing rationales and captions. We've also updated the chapter that deals with technology applications for e-portfolios.

The first two chapters set the context for portfolios. Chapter 1 provides the background, which explains how and why Constructivism makes sense in adult learning environments. In this chapter, we have expanded the explanation as to why we start the book with a discussion on human development and Constructivism. We have provided two answers to the "Why start there?" question. The first answer addresses the importance of being grounded in the knowledge base which defines early care and education as a profession. Our second answer is that portfolios are an expression of Constructivism.

Chapter 2 explains the connection between Constructivism and portfolios. This chapter now has a few small changes in word choices. The word "structural" was removed from "structural design" so that it wouldn't get confused with the addition of "structure" in Chapter 3.

In Chapter 3, *structure* has been added to the discussion on portfolio orientation, which, in the first edition, included only purpose, type, context, and audience. Structure, we discovered, was a missing component that students puzzled over. We define *structure* as answering the question, "How will components be organized?" Structure refers to the coherent organization of categories based on the criteria in use. Structure allows the builder to present a complete and articulate story.

Chapter 4, "Planning and Organizing for a Successful Portfolio," is entirely new. In this chapter we present a planning overview, then use scenarios to illustrate planning for two different types of portfolios. Scenario 1 describes a showcase portfolio; Scenario 2, an assessment portfolio. The second part of the chapter addresses organizing. Following the organizing overview, we use examples from the two scenarios to illustrate the organization process.

Chapter 5 deals with philosophy and its place in portfolio development and early care and education practice in general, and Chapter 6 provides the rationale for the practice of reflection and gives a step-by-step guide to understanding and using it effectively. These chapters have been left as is, with the exception that we adjusted the chapter numbers to accommodate the addition of the new planning/organizing chapter.

What used to be Chapter 6, "Building a Portfolio," is now Chapter 7. This chapter covers more of the nitty-gritty of portfolio work. It provides specific guidance about developing, collecting, and evaluating evidence necessary for documenting competency—a big part of what portfolios are about. This chapter has been augmented with a section that offers guidance in writing rationales and captions that accompany evidence. Through photos and examples we illustrate both effective and ineffective ways of conveying the content of artifacts. Rationale and captions were also added to the portfolio rubric. In addition to these changes, we have included the updated National Association for the Education of Young Children (NAEYC) Standards for Programs (revised 2009) and the updated California Standards for the Teaching Profession (2009).

What used to be Chapter 7, "Structure, Design, and Construction of Print and Electronic Portfolios," is now Chapter 8. This addresses the nuts and bolts of portfolio structure, design, and construction—how to show your stuff! When we wrote the first edition, we recommended the use of PowerPoint as a tool for constructing portfolios. Since then, there has been an explosion of e-portfolio software on and off the Web. After exploring a number of new options, we determined that for our students, Microsoft PowerPoint is still our preferred portfolio development tool. At this writing, PowerPoint 2010 is the most current version of the software and is an excellent tool for people who do not have a lot of technical support. We have updated information on scanning documents, using portable storage devices, and photo releases.

A major technological change that accompanies the second edition is the addition of a companion website, accessible at: www.routledge.com/textbooks/9780415800525. The website features resources for instructors and students. The instructor resources include guides for activities and lecture notes (PowerPoint slides). Student resources include strategies and instructions for navigating the portfolio development process. We provide students with templates, questions to ponder, and worksheets. Have fun exploring the site and discovering its surprises.

one
Human Development and Constructivism

We don't receive wisdom; we must discover it for ourselves after a journey that no one can take for us or spare us.

—Marcel Proust

Why Start a Book About Portfolios with Human Development and Constructivism?

There are two answers to the question "Why start a book about portfolios with human development and Constructivism?" The first answer has to do with being grounded in the knowledge base that helps define early care and education as a profession. The study of human development, child development in particular, is fundamental to best practice in early care and education (ECE). Child development and best practice are two are sides of the same coin, neither complete without the other. Our maturation as a field has brought with it widespread agreement among our ranks that ECE is, indeed, part of the education profession. There is often an unfortunate divide between practitioners who work with our youngest children (birth to kindergarten age) and those who work in early elementary education settings (K-3). In our view, we are all part of the same tapestry, all crucial parts of the educational continuum, all professionals. As such, we must assume the obligations inherent in all professions.

Across the country, ECE practitioners are discussing what professionalism means in early care and education, specifically, and how we operationalize it in programs for children and in professional preparation programs. In California, we have undertaken the task of delineating what we expect of ECE professionals by establishing the Early Childhood Educator Competencies (birth to age 5) and the California Standards for the Teaching Profession

4

(K-12). Professionalism is among the list of competencies in both of these documents. In broad strokes professionalism requires competence in a specialized body of knowledge, commitment to professional growth, professional conduct, and commitment to program improvement (California Department of Education, 2010). Understanding the roots of the ECE profession, which include the study of child development and Constructivist theory, equates to understanding substantial aspects of the field's specialized knowledge base.

The second answer to the question with which we began this chapter has to do with context. Portfolios are an expression of Constructivism, a theoretical perspective that embodies a certain way of thinking about human learning and development. Portfolios are situated within the context of Constructivism, the larger backdrop that helps define and explain the relevance of portfolios, a tool for learning, for children and adults. We believe there is value in making these connections transparent and explicit.

Constructivism

Constructivism is all about authentic learning. It explains how we come to know what we know, what it means to know something, and how our capacity to learn and what we can learn change from one stage of development to another. From an educational standpoint, it helps us understand and create the conditions that encourage and foster authentic learning.

Portfolios represent a window on authentic learning, a tool that reflects the learning process. Portfolios provide a tangible way of making sense of past and present experiences, putting learning in context, and capturing and displaying the learning that has taken place. Portfolios can facilitate authentic learning. They offer a point-in-time portrait of one's development as a learner.

In order to appreciate the power of the portfolio as a tool for learning and development, it is helpful to first understand its theoretical and philosophical foundations—the ideas, really, that underpin it and make it different from traditional forms of assessment. Strong connections exist between Constructivism as a teaching orientation and human development. A brief look at the ideas of the theorists who have so significantly influenced early childhood education provides insights into the use of pedagogy that includes portfolios.

Understanding what Constructivism is and how it differs from traditional educational philosophy sheds light on some of the difficulties many adult learners and teachers encounter when working with portfolios. It also illuminates some of the reasons that early childhood educators, who practice Constructivism in classrooms with children, have been slow to extend these practices to adult learning environments.

Constructivism: What It Is

Constructivism is considered to be a theory by some scholars, an ideology by others. Whatever descriptor you choose, two things are clear. The first is that Constructivism is a particular way of describing the nature of learning and development and how knowledge is acquired. The second is that this particular way of looking at development, learning, and knowing is at the very heart of the early care and education field.

Every discipline, and every theory within a discipline, has its own language. Familiarity with that language aids in formulating a better understanding of it. A close look at the literature on Constructivism reveals the language with which its ideas and concepts are framed and explained. Fosnot's (1996) definition provides an excellent example of the language used to discuss central concepts and ideas embedded in Constructivism. She says, "Constructivism . . . describes knowledge as temporary, developmental, nonobjective, internally constructed, and socially and culturally mediated" (p. ix).

Terms like *temporary* and *developmental* describe knowledge as something fluid and dynamic, rather than as stagnant and fixed. The words *nonobjective* and *internally constructed* denote the highly personal nature of knowledge and the active processes involved in attaining it. Concurrently, a phrase like *socially and culturally mediated* locates knowledge, and the knower, within the environments in which they live and learn. The social and cultural environments influence, and to some degree, determine or govern, what one knows and how it can be known.

Consider another part of Fosnot's (1996) definition. The language that she uses is instructive in that it clarifies the dynamics involved in learning. She describes learning as:

- a self-regulatory process of struggling with the conflict between existing personal models of the world and discrepant new insights,
- constructing new representations and models of reality as a human meaning-making venture with culturally developed tools and symbols, and
- further negotiating such meaning through cooperative social activity, discourse, and debate (p. ix).

The terms found in this and other descriptions of Constructivism signify an active stance toward learning, suggesting the learners' direct, intentional, purposeful engagement with others and the world around them. Learning is a shared activity, one that demands of us an investment of effort and time.

Where Constructivism Comes from

By world history standards, Constructivism is very young. It began in the mid-1800s and is solidly rooted in the work of Froebel, Dewey, Piaget, Vygotsky, and others. Unlike many of their contemporaries, these individuals viewed children as explorers innately disposed to actively construct knowledge and understanding of the world around them. The following brief descriptions of their ideas make clear the influence their thinking has had on early childhood programs around the world. You may recognize in them aspects of programs with which you are familiar.

Friedrich Froebel (1782–1852), influenced by the ideas of Pestalozzi, formulated play-based curriculum through which "children play their way to understanding" (Arnett, 2004, p. 10). Froebel saw children's play as symbolic and developmental, and children as active learners. He believed that "the purpose of education is to encourage and guide man as a conscious, thinking and perceiving being" (Froebel, 1826, p. 2).

John Dewey (1859–1952), the founder of progressive education, argued that children learn by engaging in meaningful, purposeful activity with real objects, doing real-life tasks, rather than by performing abstract tasks for some future purpose. He "advocated intrinsically motivating experiences as essential for the development of a united self and real understanding of subject matter" (DeVries & Kohlberg, 1990, p. 376). Dewey believed that the engagement of children's interests, abilities, capabilities, and their active nature are essential to their learning.

Dewey (1933) believed in the power and necessity of reflective thinking, which he considered an essential aim of education and what makes possible "a truly human and rational life" (pp. 17–22). Reflective thinking enables us to act in conscious, mindful ways. It allows us to consider problems and actions systematically. And it enriches and gives meaning to our lives. As with other Constructivist thinkers, Dewey emphasized active engagement in life and learning.

Piaget (1896–1980), known as the father of Constructivism, provided a theory of how intelligence develops in children and adolescents. He approached intellectual development from the perspective of invariable stage progression. His viewpoint on human development instructs us that human beings progress through specific stages, each stage marked by *a qualitative change in thinking capability*. The 4-year-old who reasons that clouds are alive because they move thinks differently than the 10-year-old who knows that a natural force acting on the clouds (wind) causes them to move. The 4-year-old generalizes actions of animate and inanimate objects (dogs move; clouds move; dogs are alive, therefore clouds must be alive). The child does not consider the wind to be a factor because the wind is not seen. The 10 to 12-year-old, however, begins to develop the capacity for hypothetical-deductive reasoning and complex and abstract thought. She can consider the nature of physical objects and more readily distinguish between what is alive and what is not. She can comprehend unseen factors, such as gravity or wind, which interact with objects, in ways the younger child cannot. With the help of concrete experiments, she can discover the effects of unseen forces on objects. For example, in a simulation of wind's effects on clouds, the child can use helium balloons tied to the backs of chairs to represent clouds, and moving air produced by a floor fan to represent wind. The child can experiment with the effects of air moving against balloons and mentally apply what she observes to phenomena that she cannot directly experience.

The 4-year-old can pretend that balloons are clouds and that the fan is making real wind. Without the cognitive structures of the older child, however, it is just pretend. There is no internalized carryover into reality. The younger child will still believe that clouds move because they are alive. The older child's more mature cognitive structures allow for a different kind of knowing in which the representations and reasoning combine to form new knowledge.

Piaget not only delineated a sequential progression of intellectual development, he explained the process by which children and adolescents learn. He used the term *adaptation* to mean learning and described the two processes that occur in learning. *Assimilation* and *accommodation* are two sides of the learning coin. Assimilation is the taking in of new information and matching it to our existing structures or ways of knowing. Accommodation is what happens when the new information does not fit into our existing mental structures or views. Accommodation requires that we transform our current view in response to the new information. The in-between condition—*disequilibrium*—results when we realize that the new information does not align with our current understanding, and we find ourselves to be temporarily off balance as we struggle to give the new information a home in our view of the world. *Equilibrium* is reached when we successfully integrate the new information, thus creating a new mental construct.

The construction of knowledge and the ideas of assimilation, accommodation, disequilibrium, and equilibrium can be illustrated by the following example.

> Jill goes to the shoe store to buy a pair of shoes. She asks for her usual size 8. The clerk brings her the size 8, which she tries on and finds to be too small. She asks for another pair, thinking that maybe the first pair was incorrectly marked. The second pair is also too small. Jill decides that that particular style doesn't work for her foot. She asks to see another style, but finds it too small as well. Jill theorizes that shoes from that particular manufacturer must run small, so asks to see other brands of shoes. Size 8 after size 8 proves to be too small, regardless of brand. Still convinced that she wears size 8, Jill applies every reason she can think of to explain why the shoes don't fit. In her attempt to reconcile this experience with her active view ("I'm a size 8"), she rationalizes, "My feet must be swollen," "It's late in the day so I must be retaining water," or "They just don't make them like they used to."

In an effort to make sense of this experience and match it with what she knows, Jill calls upon her known theories to explain it. Piaget and Inhelder (1969) describe this as assimilation, "The filtering or modification of the input" (p. 6). In other words, Jill does her best to assimilate the fact of the shoes not fitting into her current belief about her shoe size and tries to justify why she's having trouble with the size 8s.

When at last Jill cannot find a single, comfortable size 8, she's faced with having to change her mind about her shoe size. She tries on size 9 and finds that it fits perfectly. She accommodates her thinking to the current experience. Piaget and Inhelder (1969) describe this as "the modification of internal schemes to fit reality" (p. 6). This experience causes Jill to rethink her old view and create a new view. The interaction of assimilation and accommodation effectively *changes her mind*, resulting in *adaptation* (learning).

Like Dewey, Piaget believed that the construction of knowledge requires action on the part of the learner. Children do not learn from objects; rather, they learn by *acting on* objects, observing the results of those actions, and then trying to make sense of what they see. Piaget believed that the sense that children can make of their experience is limited by their stage of intellectual development. A thorough discussion of Piaget's developmental stages is beyond the scope of this book. However, we will touch on the stage Formal Operations later in this chapter in a discussion of adult learning.

Piaget primarily emphasized the *actions of the individual* in the learning process. Although he acknowledged the importance of social interaction in the construction of knowledge, it was his contemporary, Lev Vygotsky (1896–1934), who brought Social Constructivism to the forefront. Vygotsky insisted that the construction of knowledge always exists within the context of past and present social relationships. In his view, learning occurs through intentional and purposeful engagement *with more knowledgeable and experienced others* while acting on the environment. Learning and development are conditioned on human interaction and shared activity in the physical environment. As Badrova and Leong (1996) point out:

> The social context molds cognitive processes, while it is also part of the developmental process. Social context means the entire social milieu, that is, everything in the child's environment that has either been directly or indirectly influenced by the culture. (p. 9).

Vygotsky's placement of learning and development in the sociocultural context resonates with the ideas of Bronfenbrenner (1917–2005), who sets human development within the context of an ecological system. In Bronfenbrenner's model, the child is, first and foremost, part of a microsystem—the family. Each individual and each relationship within the family affects the others. As the child develops, he experiences the larger environment—the mesosystem—in which he, and his family members, interact with, for example, extended family, child care, school, the neighborhood, and the church. The relationships represented in these and other microsystems directly influence the child's development and worldview. In less direct ways, yet important ones, the child is affected by elements in the exosystem, such as the parents' work, the school board, government agencies, the legal system, and other entities with which family members have contact. And finally, the child is influenced, again indirectly, by the macrosystem, or global context, which includes, for instance, cultural customs, social class, historical events, and popular ideologies.

The Other Side of Human Development

Constructivism tells an important story about the social and cognitive aspects of, and conditions for, learning. It is not the whole story, however. The Child Study Movement, begun by G. Stanley Hall (1844–1924), "was dedicated to creating a scientific approach to understanding child development" (Frost, Wortham, & Reifel, 2005, p. 14). The idea of the *whole child* was born in that movement, and it forms an important part of the foundation on which Constructivism is built. The concept of the *whole person*—both the cognitive and affective aspects—has been fundamental to the larger study of human development.

While Dewey, Piaget, and others were busy investigating cognitive development and learning, Sigmund Freud (1856–1939) was revolutionizing the way we think about the structure and development of the psyche or mental life of the person. He hypothesized that the psyche is made up of three interacting aspects: *id*—our instincts; *ego*—"the intermediary between id and the external world" (Strachey, 1969, p. 2); and *superego*—our conscience. Freud illuminated the workings of the unconscious mind—our motivations, drives, interpretations of reality, and desires—which influence our conscious and unconscious choices throughout life.

The theories of Freud and his student, Eric Erikson (1902–1994), have provided insights into the development and functioning of the affective domain. They identified psychosexual and psychosocial stages, respectively, through which individuals internalize and make emotional and social-psychological sense out of their experiences. Our interpretations of the experiences in each stage provide either a healthy foundation for development that continues with us throughout life, or one that is, to some degree, compromised. The extent to which we successfully resolve the issues in each stage

affects the quality and stability of the stages that follow, and have a conse-
quent effect on the quality of our lives and subsequent relationships. These
theories address the effects of the individual's *personal interactions* with
significant others within each stage. For instance, during infancy, the quality of the infant's life experience depends on the mother's level and quality
of responsiveness to the infant's needs. Healthy development requires that
the infant's efforts to communicate be met with timely, nurturing, appropriate responses. A consistent pattern of responsiveness convinces the infant
on an unconscious level that the world is a safe place, that relationships
are satisfying, that she is competent to communicate her needs, and that
her needs will be met. In Erikson's (1963) terms, she forms a basic sense
of trust, rather than one of mistrust. It is postulated that these formative
experiences throughout childhood have a profound impact on our adult
lives, influencing everything from the spouse we choose to the feelings and
thoughts we experience when we enter a room full of strangers.

When viewed in combination, this sample of theories presents a picture
of development that views the human being as possessing both a conscious
and unconscious mind, which is shaped through a combination of genetic
endowments and direct and indirect social experiences. Each domain inter-
acts with and affects the development of the other; each is important to
healthy development. Individual strengths and challenges are manifested in
various ways and are influenced by a multitude of personal and environmen-
tal factors. Our emotional and cognitive lives are intertwined. Piaget and
Inhelder (1969) noted the reciprocal and inseparable nature of our cognitive
and affective sides. They concluded that every pattern of behavior, no matter
how intellectual, is always influenced to some degree by our affective states.
Conversely, our affective states have voice—in fact, exist—as a result of our
cognitive structures. This holds true for both children and adults.

Much of the early care and education field reflects these Constructivist,
psychodynamic, and ecological views of learning and development. We can
see the reflections of Dewey, Piaget, Vygotsky, Freud, Erikson, Bronfenbrenner, and others in our field in how we view young children, and in how
these views are expressed in high-quality early childhood programs. Early
childhood educators respect children's capacities and emerging capabilities.
We view their learning as a complex, personal, and interpersonal endeavor
with both emotional and cognitive content. We give children opportunities,
in a social context, to express and examine their thoughts and knowledge
about the world as they experience it. Against the backdrop of their understanding and capabilities at a given time, we engage them with new opportunities that challenge and invite them to try out, and think about, their
thinking and actions in response to what they have learned—to continually
transform their knowledge in synchrony with their expanding capabilities.
We also take into consideration their feelings, motivations, desires, and

psychological needs. Learning requires that children actively engage in a potent, circular process that includes action on objects and ideas, interaction with more knowledgeable others, and reflection and dialogue on their thinking and actions in supportive environments. We understand children's learning as a transformative process. This is not only true for children, however. It is also true for adults. Why, then, do we so rarely find Constructivist ideas and practices at work in adult learning environments?

Why Our Teaching Practices in Adult Learning Environments Often Do Not Reflect Our Constructivist Beliefs

Although many early childhood educators share these human development views and embrace and practice Constructivism with children, there has been a long-standing disconnect in the early care and education field between how we teach adults and how we teach adults to work with children. Two factors may explain the pervasive disconnect that results in the perpetuation of *teaching as telling* in the adult classroom.

The first factor has its roots in the history of our educational system. Our educational institutions are historically underpinned by a philosophical ideology referred to as *cultural transmission*, which stems from the Behaviorist tradition. Prior to the 1800s, conventional wisdom held that children were empty vessels to be filled up by adults. John Locke (1632–1704) wrote, "the mind of a newborn infant is like a blank page upon which experience writes" (Harriman, 1941, pp. 180–181). Locke coined the phrase *tabula rasa* to describe this idea. *Tabula rasa* is associated with Behaviorism wherein it is believed that experience *acts on the child* to produce learning. In this view, knowledge results when information comes from the outside to the inside through the senses. External stimuli govern what can be known, and therefore, learned (DeVries & Kohlberg, 1990). Behaviorism acknowledges only that which comes from outside the person, that which is observable and measurable. It makes no allowance for the unseen mental activity of the person through which one *acts on, shapes, comprehends, invents, and makes meaning from and within* one's environment and experience. Harriman (1941) illustrates this Behaviorist premise as he explains, "If the infant were incapable of receiving and responding to stimuli, and of acquiring new modes of responses, there would be nothing of what we call mind or mental development" (p. 182).

In the cultural transmission view, children learn by having adults transmit information to them; this is a view that sees children as passive receptacles who take as their own, without question or reflection, that which others know, say, or believe. If we consider the cultural transmission ideology—

which conceives of learning as a passive activity—we can see that it is an approach that persists in much of elementary, secondary, and adult education. Hillocks (1999) describes this passive approach as an *objectivist stance* to teaching, that is, "teaching . . . as an act of telling" (p. 93). With such an approach, it is not difficult to understand why the lecture method is so common in our collective school experience. It makes sense if learning is thought of as an exercise in filling the heads of students with information poured from the mouths of teachers. It also assumes that information is something to be wholly transmitted, static and permanent by nature, requiring nothing more than absorption on the part of the learner.

Through our extensive personal experiences in school, we have each formed beliefs and theories about the nature of teaching and learning. These beliefs and theories contain powerful, enduring ideas about authority relationships, teachers' roles and responsibilities, pedagogy, and the roles we, and our peers, play in relation to our learning. If we predominantly experienced traditional methods of education, chances are good that we hold the unconscious, fundamental assumptions that teachers possess knowledge and then transmit it to students (Bullard, 2003), that learning occurs through the passive transfer of knowledge from teacher to student, and that students are the recipients of that knowledge "who perform according to the teachers' expectations" (Burk & Dunn, 1996, p. 11). Motivation for learning results from the external rewards bestowed on the student by the teacher. These rewards most often take the form of grades.

If we experienced a passive educational approach as our primary mode of instruction, then it may be the mode that "feels right" to us, even though we might have experienced it as ineffective—that is, the information we heard did not stick. As teachers, we have often heard students say, "I learned it for the test. As soon as the test was over, I forgot everything." In spite of this fairly constant refrain, educators of adults persist in using a passive approach, because it is, after all, what we know, and that with which we are most comfortable. Bullard (2003) cites extensive research that confirms that the personal theories learners hold about teaching and learning, their beliefs about the proper roles of teachers and students, and the ideas they maintain about the right way to teach and learn are, indeed, highly resistant to change. Furthermore, these beliefs act as a filter when a learner is confronted with new ways of doing things, often confounding the possibility of change.

A second factor that may contribute to early childhood educators' perpetuation of *teaching as telling* is how we have understood and interpreted Piaget's stage of Formal Operations. As stated previously, Piaget was a stage theorist. He believed that children mature into each of four stages—Formal Operations being the last—and that each stage builds upon those that precede it. No stage can be skipped. Each stage is marked by distinct states of intellectual capability. Developing intellect is not a matter of learning more;

it is a matter of growing the capability for more sophisticated thought processes. In other words, the way that children are able to think is fundamentally different from the way adults are able to think.

So how might our interpretation of this stage contribute to *teaching as telling*? The hallmark of Piaget's stage of Formal Operations is the development of capabilities for abstract and complex thought, metacognition (thinking about thinking), and hypothetical-deductive reasoning (Arnett, 2004). In Formal Operations, ideas, rather than concrete objects, become the prominent currency. We know that both language and ideas are abstract, and inextricably linked. Many of us have been taught that *all* adolescents and adults achieve, and engage in, Formal Operations as a matter of inevitable stage progression, as Piaget suggested. If we believe that all adolescents and adults think in abstract and complex ways, and that they understand language—a system of abstract symbols that conveys meaning—then why would not we also believe that these learners can absorb and understand, by being "told," what we expect them to know?

These two factors—our experiences as passive learners and our beliefs about how adults learn—conspire to keep us blind to change. They keep our *quiet theories* about education, internalized through years of experience, in place. It is those quiet theories that provide our personal recipes for educational practice. The most common recipe in our schools today is based on the notion of passing on wholly formed knowledge to students, who learn, not through action and social interaction, but instead through rote memorization and didactic instructional methods.

The Constructivist view of learning invites us to challenge our quiet theories about teaching and learning. Arnett (2004) cites abundant research that gives us a revised view of Piaget's stage of Formal Operations. That research indicates that, rather than a certainty into which all people mature, Formal Operations is a universal potential that all people possess. That potential is realized and exercised differently in different cultures. The ways in which it is developed and exercised is determined by the cognitive tasks on which individual cultures depend. People tend to exercise their capability for abstract and complex thought selectively, often with problems with which they are most familiar or with which they have the most experience. People who have had systematic or specialized training are more likely than others to develop their capabilities for abstract and complex thought. Those who develop these capabilities often use them selectively or inconsistently. Some fail to exercise this level of thought at all. In short, we must be taught to think abstractly and reflectively, engage in guided practice to become proficient, and exert considerable effort and energy to exercise this kind of thinking effectively in our daily lives.

In describing a Constructivist stance toward teaching and learning, Hillocks (1999) says:

Teachers cannot simply tell students what is to be learned and expect them to learn it . . . students must themselves be active agents in their own learning, transforming what is to be learned through the screen of their own experience and existing understandings . . . to be successful, learners must construct or reconstruct, for themselves, what is to be learned (p. 93).

We contend that this is true for both the child and the adult learner.

How Constructivism Applies to Adult Learners

Early childhood educators have focused primarily on how Constructivism applies to children and on how to put into operation Constructivist ideas to build meaningful curriculums in children's programs. A great deal has been written about adult development, learning, and education, and the connections among them, in the past few decades, however. Educators such as Mezirow (1990, 1991, 2000), Brookfield (1986, 1987, 1995, 1996), and Candy (1991) have echoed the ideas of the early Constructivists and extended Constructivist principles to adult environments. These prominent adult educators view learning as potentially emancipatory and transformative. Their work, and that of others in the field of adult education, is replete with references to active learning, self-direction, and intrinsic motivation.

Our own experiences with a wide variety of adults and children in diverse learning environments have taught us that Constructivism and the pedagogical practices that it suggests apply equally well to students of any age. As with children, adults tend to thrive in settings that invite and value their active, purposeful participation, and where learning is a shared responsibility. Most adults respond to an atmosphere of inquiry, wherein their questions about, and exploration of, the world and themselves are encouraged. We have discovered that high-level learning is most likely to occur when teachers and students engage, with open minds, in productive and energetic dialogue and meaningful tasks that address real problems.

Constructivism has given us an alternative to the cultural transmission approach to learning. In doing so, it gives us guidance as to the role of education. Daloz (1999) says, "The proper aim of education is to promote significant learning. Significant learning entails development. Development means successively asking broader and deeper questions of the relationship between oneself and the world" (p. 3). The connection that Daloz makes between learning and development is a crucial one, but to early childhood educators, not an unfamiliar one. If Daloz were talking in Piagetian terms, she would be discussing the process of assimilation and accommodation, which results in adaptation (learning). As you recall, in this process, we first try to interpret new information using our existing ways of knowing. Upon finding the existing structures inadequate, we construct a new way of understanding and making sense of the experience—our ways of knowing are transformed. The adult learning literature underscores and corroborates Piaget's analysis of how learning happens, not only in children, but in adults as well. Ultimately, what Piaget described is the process of *transformative human* learning.

The Constructivist view of learning moves us from a perspective of learning as *transfer of information* to one of learning as *transformation of information.* An educational approach that is built on *information transfer* often results in surface learning and an assortment of discrete bits of information with a short shelf life. For example, most of us took a course in geometry in high school. We were instructed to memorize theorem after theorem. We may have done so and successfully passed every exam. Can we recall and employ a single one when trying to figure out how many square feet an odd-shaped piece of ground contains when planning the school garden?

On the other hand, an educational approach built on *information transformation* has the potential for resulting in deep-level learning with staying power. Why? Because when we transform information, truly learn it, we make it our own. It becomes knowledge. If we had really learned the theorems in geometry class, rather than temporarily memorized them, we would understand their underlying principles and the processes through which they were derived. We would have made sense of them by struggling with their meaning, applying them in varied circumstances, observing and analyzing our results, and sharing and comparing the results with others. Through this active, involved collaborative process, we would have altered our pre-theorem world understanding to a more enlightened one that includes our working knowledge of theorems as a way of understanding how the world operates. That transformed information—knowledge—would then be available to us when planning the school garden!

Implications for the Adult Learning Environment

Constructivist principles orient us toward a dynamic educational environment for adult learners. As educators of adults, our desire to reinvent our teaching in ways that bring what we do, what we know, and what we believe into harmony has given us the courage and impetus to experiment, reflect, engage in dialogue, study, and experiment some more. We have recognized that upsetting the apple cart, so to speak, has risks for us as teachers and for our students as well. Not only have we experienced the discomfort of jarring our own ideas about teaching and learning, but we have also encountered resistance and anxiety in our students as we bring Constructivist principles to bear in our classrooms. To some extent, we are all prisoners of our *quiet theories*. On the printed page, the idea of *cognitive conflict* or *dissonance* sounds rather benign and intellectual. In practice, it often causes emotional and intellectual confusion, rebellion, foot-dragging, avoidance, and anger in students. Most of them rise to the challenge. Many times, students embrace the adventure and engage wholeheartedly, becoming learning partners with us in the co-construction of knowledge. Our efforts to operationalize Constructivism in the adult classroom continue to inform our practice as teachers, and open cognitive doors for adult learners that help them transform their thinking, knowing, and doing. We see this when they grapple with issues, scaffold one another's learning, try out and analyze new approaches to old problems, and reflect on their efforts and progress. We see the practice of Constructivist principles come to life when adult learners make visible what they know, how they know it, what they can do, and what it all means to them.

In the next chapter, we explore Constructivism as it relates specifically to portfolios. Our journeys to discovering better ways to teach have brought us, by different paths, to portfolios. In them, we have found more than the stories of students' learning. We have found an important part of our Constructivist selves.

A Final Note

Constructivism is at the heart of early care and education. If offers a holistic view of human learning and development, considering the cognitive, social, and affective aspects of the learner. Although, ECE practitioners characteristically apply Constructivist principles and practices to working with children, the same practices and principles are not always extended to adult learners. However, the theoretical basis and implications for practice embedded in Constructivism apply equally well to both children and adults.

two
How Portfolios Reflect Constructivism

The self is not something ready-made, but something in continuous formation through choice of action.

—John Dewey

Constructivism and Portfolios

In traditional schooling, emphasis has been placed squarely, and almost exclusively, on development in the cognitive domain. Educators expend proportionately little energy, in an intentional, concerted way, on development in the affective and social domains. The single-minded focus on logical-mathematical and linguistic skills, and the testing that accompanies it, might lead one to believe that knowing facts and learning to manage, process, and express information makes for an educated person. Behaviorism, so fundamental to and deeply ingrained in our education system, undergirds this view. While there is no question that cognitive skill-building and retaining information are important, they represent only one dimension of learning. Hutchings and Wutzdorff (1988) describe learning, in part, as involving and engaging a range of domains, including the cognitive, kinesthetic, affective, ethical, attitudinal, and behavioral. As educators, if we recognize the logical-mathematical and linguistic biases embedded in our educational institutions, and perhaps in our own quiet theories, and we begin to think about learning as going beyond these dimensions of cognition, then we must ask ourselves what else is important in adult learning, and how is it realized? These are some of the connections and questions we continually consider as we reflect on our practice with adult learners.

In order to bring about change, we had to reexamine what we believe about how people develop and learn. We challenged our own theories about education and educational practice. We wanted an approach wherein the learning and developmental needs of the whole person are considered. It meant moving away from a didactic stance—*teaching as telling*—*learning as receiving*—into a position of *facilitator of learning and development*—*active participant*. The *teaching as telling*—*learning as receiving* approach is conducive to the idea of "knowledge as facts." A *facilitator of learning and development*—*active participant* approach invites a different understanding of knowledge, and a different approach to knowledge-building. It is one that treats education as a partnership. It is respectful of what the learner, as well as the teacher, brings to the educational environment. It includes both the cognitive and affective aspects of the learner.

Through his theory of Multiple Intelligences, Howard Gardner (1983) introduced the idea that intelligence is not limited to the logical-mathematical or linguistic arenas. Rather, intelligence finds expression in a variety of "frames of mind" that also include the musical, kinesthetic, naturalistic, spatial, intrapersonal, and interpersonal (p. 8). Daniel Goleman (1995) argues that emotional intelligence contributes immeasurably to human success. The emotional mind and the rational mind, he explains, present "two fundamentally different ways of knowing [which] interact to construct our mental life" (p. 8). Often, he says, "these minds are exquisitely coordinated; feelings are essential to thought, thought to feeling" (p. 9). Emotional intelligence encompasses empathy, self-awareness, personal motivation, and a host of other aspects that enable us to engage with ourselves and with others to succeed in personal relationships, work, and play. Our experience has taught us that it is not enough to engage our adult students cognitively. As Mezirow (2000) points out, "transformative learning is more than rationally based; it relies on the affective dimension of knowing" (p. 303).

A teaching/learning approach that takes into account the cognitive, social, and affective dimensions of the learner necessitates the use of tools, methods, and strategies that go well beyond the standard paper-and-pencil tests and the traditional emphasis on "producing the right answer." Examination of our practice prompted us to explore alternative approaches that would facilitate, in adult learners, the messy kind of learning we observe in young children—exploratory, inventive, insightful, and productive. We wanted to find ways to engage adult learners in developing competencies, enabling them "*to resolve genuine problems or difficulties* . . . to create an effective product [that entails] the potential for *finding or creating problems*—thereby laying the groundwork for the acquisition of new knowledge" (Gardner, 1983, pp. 60–61). We were seeking to engage students in what Fosnot (1996) describes as "an interpretive, recursive, building process by active learners interacting with the physical and social world" (p. 30). Portfolios provided us with a powerful strategy and tool with which to engage students.

FIGURE 2.1 Conceptual Alignment

Figure 2.1 illustrates the alignments between theory and practice with which we struggled to arrive at internal congruence and consistency in our teaching. It shows the interplay between theories (how people learn and develop) and philosophy (beliefs and values about how best to educate them). Pedagogy (how teachers teach) emanates from theories and beliefs. If theories and beliefs are aligned, pedagogical choices tend to be more clear and consistent. In fact, theoretical and philosophical groundings influence pedagogical approach. In our case, bringing our theories and philosophy into alignment caused us to reframe our pedagogy. Portfolios emerged as a pedagogical response to that realignment. This is the same alignment struggle we have observed taking place in our adult students as they move through the portfolio process. In effect, the portfolio process has set up the dynamic, whereby students are called to question their theories, beliefs, and practices.

Our Journey to Portfolios: A Constructivist Story

The past few decades have seen a dramatic increase in the use of portfolios in schools of education to assess the preparation of elementary, middle, and secondary school teachers, and also at the college and university levels as tools for determining readiness for tenure and promotion. Although early childhood educators have become accustomed to using portfolios in their classrooms to document children's growth and development, portfolios are much less often used with adult learners in early childhood course preparation and continuing education programs. We find this particularly curious, in that, as previously noted, early childhood educators have long been committed to the Constructivist philosophy in working with children. Constructivism has been an ideal in early care and education to a much greater degree, and for a much longer time, than at any other level of American education.

It is clear from our observations of good early childhood practice that early childhood educators, in the spirit of Constructivism, understand and respond to the uneven growth and development patterns in young children. They expect and plan for the messiness of children's learning. They encourage their creativity, actively engage them, challenge them, and scaffold their learning, and consider both their cognitive and affective needs. Educators sometimes forget, however, that all of these things also apply when dealing with adult learners.

What Are Portfolios?

There are many definitions of portfolios in the education literature (Brown & Wolfe-Quintero, 1997; Campbell, Cignetti, Melenyzer, Nettles, & Wyman, 2004; Cerbin, 1994; Paulson, Paulson, & Meyer, 1991; Wolf & Dietz, 1998; Wolf, Lichtenstein & Stevenson, 1997). They generally characterize portfolios as organized or structured collections of work compiled for a specific purpose related to the demonstration of one's learning, skills, and accomplishments. Most of the definitions refer only to the portfolio product—that is, the end result of a series of steps. Others make explicit the process aspect of portfolio development—process as it relates to personal change (McMillan, 2004; Wilcox, 1996; Wolf & Dietz, 1998). Some of the definitions emphasize the role of reflection in portfolios (Wolf & Dietz, 1998; Wolf et al., 1997), while others are silent on this point.

As we have come to better understand the complexity of portfolios through our work with students, our definition has evolved. In it, we have tried to capture both the process and the product dimensions of portfolios, which we see as being intertwined and complementary. The process that underlies portfolio development is as important as the product itself, as it is through the process that learning occurs. The quality and depth of the process is reflected in the product, and ultimately determines the quality of the product. This, then, is our definition:

> Portfolios are rich, contextual, highly personalized documentaries of one's learning journey. They contain purposefully organized documentation that clearly demonstrates specific knowledge, skills, dispositions and accomplishments achieved over time. Portfolios represent connections made between actions and beliefs, thinking and doing, and evidence and criteria. They are a medium for reflection through which the builder constructs meaning, makes

the learning process transparent and learning visible, crystallizes insights, and anticipates future direction.

Portfolios represent both an expression of Constructivist learning and a vehicle for Constructivist practice. Portfolios are the embodiment of holistic learning. The process learners experience in developing portfolios, and the products that result, allow them, and invite them, to give voice to their cognitive, social, and affective selves. Portfolios are portraits of their builders.

Portfolios lend themselves to a variety of uses that we will discuss in later chapters. In all cases, however, they facilitate learners' exploring of questions and addressing of problems that are complex, multifaceted, reflective of builders' value systems, and embedded in the sociocultural environment. Portfolios represent an approach to learning wherein the "right answer" is not the teacher's answer, but rather one constructed by the learner in dialogue with others.

Characteristics of Portfolios

All portfolios hold several common characteristics, which we briefly discuss below with a reference to where in the book we cover them in detail.

Clearly Specified Purpose and Audience

The purpose and audience of the portfolio must be clearly defined and understood. Purpose and audience guide the builder in decision making with regard to collection, use, and presentation of evidence. Purpose and audience suggest the type of portfolio that is most appropriate and may indicate a particular design. We cover purpose and audience in detail in Chapter 3.

Philosophy Statement

All portfolios contain some form of philosophy statement. This carefully crafted statement unifies all elements within the portfolio. It embodies one's beliefs and values, which underpin and center the process. Chapter 5 discusses philosophy statements in detail.

Reflections

Reflection is the defining characteristic of portfolios. None is complete without it. It is what separates a portfolio from a scrapbook. Reflections tie artifacts to learning and provide evidence of growth and change over time. Reflection is covered in detail in Chapter 6.

Evidence

Evidence must be carefully selected and suited to the portfolio's purpose. Selecting documentation is akin to furnishing a room. If done poorly, without planning and reflection, the room can look like grandma's unkempt attic. If done well, it can convey a sense of balance, harmony, style, and substance—a place where one (the reader) would want to spend time. Evidence is addressed in depth in Chapter 7.

Design

Design is all about the packaging of the final product. It involves such issues as format and organization of the document as a whole. The decisions you make here will determine how the work is received and will allow your personality to shine through. Design is discussed in detail in Chapter 8.

Benefits of Portfolio Development

In our experience, portfolio development has benefited adult learners in some significant ways. First, the portfolio process helps students to reframe how they see themselves as learners. It empowers individuals to take responsibility for their learning—to examine previously passive roles and to become more proactive in their learning endeavors. It encourages them to think about their learning, and the learning environment, in critical and meaningful ways—to become mindful, intentional, self-directed learners. For many learners, the portfolio process reignites their intellectual curiosity, the same quality we admire and seek to foster in children.

Second, the portfolio process provokes adult learners to look at education differently—as integrative and ongoing—reaching far beyond the confines of the classroom and continuing throughout life. We have heard so often from students over the years that they have felt that their college classes were irrelevant and had no connection to "real life." Many have experienced higher education as a series of hoops one jumps through to get the "piece of paper." On the contrary, students who have experienced the portfolio process report a high degree of connectedness between what they do in the college classroom with what they experience beyond the classroom door. The real-world nature of portfolio work bridges the theory-to-practice gap in ways that result in meaningful learning and change. Course content ceases to be the stuff one crams for a test and soon forgets. It comes to be owned by the learner, and therefore it becomes part of the fabric of one's professional life and development.

Third, portfolio development encourages meaningful, rather than rote, learning. This kind of learning rarely happens in a straight line. It involves inevitable twists and turns, requires backsteps, and goes around corners only to confront and challenge the learner in new and unexpected ways. It is the messy kind of learning that requires all of us, teachers and students, to think about and question what we know, how we know it, and how it affects us, and it requires that we engage in dialogue about these things together. Grant and Huebner (1998) call this "powerful learning . . . active and relevant. In teacher education, as in all educational settings, powerful learning happens when what is learned and how it is learned are organized to build on the strengths of the learner" (pp. 33–34). Fink (2003) calls it significant learning.

Fink (2003) has provided a taxonomy of significant learning that we think finds expression in the process of portfolio development, and in the product itself. He describes significant learning experiences as those that have "both a *process* and an *outcome* dimension" (p. 6). In his view, and ours, significant learning results in lasting change that the learner interprets as important and meaningful in his personal or professional life. Fink identifies six kinds of significant learning that involve the cognitive, social, and emotional domains: foundational knowledge, application, integration, human dimension, caring, and learning how to learn (p. 30). Figure 2.2 provides our interpretation of his taxonomy as we use it with our students.

As Fink (2003) points out,

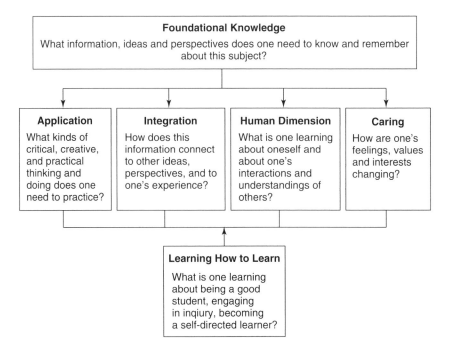

FIGURE 2.2 Taxonomy of Significant Learning

One important feature of this taxonomy is that it is not hierarchical but rather relational and even interactive . . . each kind of learning is related to the other kinds of learning and . . . achieving any one kind of learning simultaneously enhances the possibility of achieving the other kinds of leaning as well (p. 32).

Notice that the process begins with foundational knowledge—what one sets out to learn, for example, about the relationship between child development, play, and learning. It is not enough to learn the names of Smilansky's play states in children from birth to age 5. The other kinds of learning—application, integration, the human dimension, and caring—are the aspects that help transform the information into personal knowledge that has meaning. The ability to apply the knowledge—to recognize solitary play and differentiate it from parallel play while observing a group of children—provides new tools that help one be more effective in designing play opportunities and in being more responsive to children's individual play needs. Integrating our understanding of block play and our knowledge of how children develop spatial reasoning and literacy enlarges one's repertoire of curriculum tools. Looking closely at children's play in relation to their development gives one an opportunity to examine one's beliefs and attitudes about the importance and purpose of play. This human dimension of learning gives insights into the messages one gives parents, children, and others about the place play has in education. The caring aspect of learning invites us to fall in love with a subject like play, or perhaps come to value it in a way previously unfelt. And finally, experiencing learning in this holistic way opens the door to more self-directed learning.

As Fink (2003) points out, learning is interconnected. An interactive, relational approach predisposes consideration of both the cognitive and affective domains in the learning process. Portfolios engage students by invoking their cognitive and affective involvement.

Fourth, our experience has shown that portfolio development strengthens formal operational thought processes—metacognition, abstract and complex thought, and hypothetical-deductive reasoning. It provides not only a means for internalizing learning at deeper levels, but also a means for developing and/or refining higher order thinking skills. As pointed out in Chapter 1, higher order skills, characteristic of the Formal Operations stage of development, do not just happen. They are realized through a combination of an individual's cognitive readiness, systematic instruction, and guided practice, along with an individual's personal effort. Grant and Huebner (1998) point out that "Learning with understanding is more likely when one is required to explain, elaborate, or defend one's position to others, as well as one's self" (p. 35). Portfolios necessitate a complex interplay of activities in which the learner is constantly striving to explain, elaborate, and defend. They provide a vehicle through which learners transform information and experience into new knowledge that becomes their own, and think contextually about thinking and learning in increasingly complex ways.

Fifth, portfolio development facilitates self-awareness and discovery. It encourages learners to express what they know and can do in personally meaningful, individualized, and creative ways. Portfolios accommodate multiple ways of knowing and acknowledge the full range of learning styles. Portfolios often validate learners' knowledge and skills, encouraging them to reflect on, recognize, evaluate, and appreciate their own progress. They are a vehicle for refining professional identity and recording ongoing growth, and they provide a source of pride for the builder.

Challenging Aspects of Portfolio Development

Portfolio development presents adult learners with a variety of challenges. First, it is time consuming. The concept of adult portfolios is new to many students and consequently takes time to fully understand. Portfolios require considerable planning, collection and development of evidence, organization, and assembly—all of which take time. They demand a high degree of stick-to-itiveness, self-pacing, follow-through, and attention to detail.

Second, for many students, portfolios can be anxiety producing, at least initially. The highly individualized nature of portfolios makes them unlike most other kinds of assignments with which students are familiar. They represent a shift from teacher-directed to student-directed learning that can cause psychological disequilibrium—a quake in one's quiet theories about teachers' and students' roles in the learning environment and what learning is. A certain measure of discomfort accompanies any significant learning, any significant shift in how one experiences learning, and any significant shift in external expectations surrounding learning. The disequilibrium that these shifts bring about, however, also creates the possibility for substantive growth and change.

Third, portfolio development can be unsettling because it requires reconsideration of one's thinking about the nature and purpose of adult learning. What early childhood educators believe about children's learning—that it is a messy, uneven process that requires tenacity—is also true for adults. Instead of messing around with sand and water, adults mess around with ideas. The process is the same; only the medium has changed. It takes a while to get back in the habit of being curious, inventive, and intuitive where learning is concerned. It takes time, effort, and trust to unlearn years of passivity—to go from "What does the teacher want?" to "What will help me develop as a professional?"

And finally, portfolio development challenges adult learners to develop, and then utilize and trust, their own instincts and judgment. Instincts and judgment must be exercised in a whole range of decisions, such as what artifact is meaningful and important in relation to a particular criterion, when is something enough or too much, what constitutes quality, and how can one best project professionalism.

The challenges students face in developing portfolios may seem daunting at first. The anxiety, confusion, and uncertainty students sometimes feel are certainly very real, and very predictable. It has been our experience, however, and students have reported to us, that the benefits far outweigh the negatives. The autonomy students feel, the uniqueness of each student's experience, and the true sense of ownership and accomplishment that comes with the portfolio territory makes it all worth it in the end. For many, it is truly a transforming experience.

A Final Note

Portfolios open a window into the learning process. They offer a dynamic alternative to more traditional approaches to learning. They give students opportunities to explore and experiment with real-world problems and demonstrate what they know and can do. Without a doubt, portfolios are time consuming and require a great deal of effort to do well, but the outcome—and the learning that results from it—are lasting.

three
Portfolio Orientation

Purpose, Type, Context, Structure, and Audience

Learning is not attained by chance, it must be sought for with ardor and attended to with diligence.

—Abigail Adams

Just as an architect must "get the lay of the land" before planning a project and laying the first brick, the portfolio builder must understand the orientation before embarking on the building of a portfolio. Orientation refers to the portfolio's purpose, the type of portfolio best suited to the purpose, the context in which it will be used, the structure suggested by a particular criteria, and the intended audience. Purpose, type, context, structure, and audience set the orientation of the portfolio and give the builder direction.

In our review of the literature on portfolios, we have found that the terms *purpose, type*, and *audience* are often confused, lumped together, or used interchangeably. The idea of *context* is rarely addressed. Structure tends to be approached as a one-size-fits-all. In our work, we have given each of these terms specific meaning as they relate to this notion of portfolio orientation. We distinguish between the *purposes* for which portfolios are developed, the *types* of portfolios one might develop, the *audiences* to whom they are directed, the *contexts* in which they are commonly employed, and the *structures* that follow from criteria, as these are not the same.

28

Purpose, Type, Context, Structure, and Audience: What is the Difference?

We think about portfolios in this way: One develops a particular type of portfolio to achieve a specific purpose within a context that includes an identified audience. Purpose and type are closely related, as are context and audience.

Purpose answers the question "Why am I doing this?" It is the reason for which a portfolio is created. Purpose is central to everything that follows in both development and design of a portfolio. Purpose determines the type of portfolio to be developed and indicates the likely audience to whom it will be directed.

Type answers the question "What kind of portfolio is best suited to the purpose?" The type of portfolio you develop flows directly from its purpose. We distinguish four basic types of portfolios, as we use them. These types are developmental, showcase, assessment, and professional portfolios.

Context answers the question "How and where will I use it?" We define *contexts* as the circumstances or situations in which portfolios are used. For instance, you may develop a portfolio as a course or program requirement wherein the instructor directs and guides the process and sets the parameters.

Structure answers the question "How will components be organized?" Structure refers to the coherent organization of categories based on the criteria in use. Structure allows the builder to present a complete and articulate story.

Audience answers the question "To whom is this portfolio directed?" Audience refers to the person or persons for whom the portfolio is produced— that is, the primary reader or readers of the portfolio. Typically, portfolios are tailored to fit the requirements indicated by a particular audience, such as an instructor, an employer, or a certification board. Specific audiences are assumed in given contexts. Different audiences expect and look for different things. Identifying and understanding these requirements and expectations is part of the portfolio builder's initial challenge.

The following examples illustrate the relationships among elements—purpose, type, context, structure, and audience—that constitute the portfolio orientation. If, for instance, the purpose is to provide a basis for evaluation in the context of a job search, a professional portfolio will be structured to highlight requirements. The audience will be the individual, panel, or committee conducting the interview. A second use of portfolios with the purpose of providing a basis for evaluation is found in a college course. An assessment portfolio may be used to demonstrate what you have learned and can do in relation to the subject matter and skills specified in the course. The primary audience will be the instructor.

A Closer Look at Purpose

Purpose is central to the portfolio process, a kind of guiding beacon. Every aspect of the portfolio project should clearly connect to the purpose. Wolf and Dietz (as cited in Bartell, Kaye, & Morin, 1998) point out that "the portfolio purpose is instrumental in shaping the form, content, and process of the portfolio" (p. 7). We find that there are three general purposes that portfolios serve. They are used to:

1. facilitate and chart development,
2. provide a basis for evaluation, and
3. highlight performance and capabilities.

It is important to note that these purposes need not be mutually exclusive, although each can stand alone. Each purpose is valuable in and of itself. Any of the purposes may initially be the primary driving force behind the development of a portfolio. Portfolios are not one-size-fits-all documents, nor is a single portfolio intended to meet the needs of every audience. Instead, they are tailored to fit specific needs for specific purposes. If constructed with care, they are easily adapted. Adaptation may involve additions, deletions, reformulation, or reconfiguration of materials. With adaptation, however, a portfolio may serve several purposes over time and be used in different contexts. In all cases, as stand-alone, single-purpose documents or as sequential-use documents, they must remain congruent with your philosophy, which is reflective of who you are. We think of portfolios as having the potential for being living documents that can develop and mature with their builders throughout their careers. Although we have seen very few references to this notion of multiple, sequential purposes in the literature, we have found it useful and applicable in a variety of adult and higher education settings. Here are a couple of examples of multiple, sequential purposes.

In a degree completion option in child development at our university, students create comprehensive program portfolios. Their portfolios are intended from the outset to accomplish two purposes: (1) to demonstrate professional competency in relation to National Association for the Education of Young Children (NAEYC) Standards for Programs over the course of a 43-unit program, and (2) to highlight performance and capabilities through integrated projects designed to improve practice. Each portfolio entry represents a significant activity or product that the students (full-time working professionals in early care and education settings) have developed and implemented at their work sites or in the professional community. Each portfolio entry embodies and illustrates their learning in multiple content areas (e.g., curriculum, working with diverse families, advocacy). The portfolio in its entirety provides a portrait of the students' holistic learning and accomplishments relative to the program curriculum. At the conclusion of the program, many students adapt their portfolios to a second purpose—to provide a basis for evaluation. The original portfolios often constitute the basis for professional portfolios, which they develop at a later date.

Another example of multiple, sequential purposes is seen in an option within the teaching credential program. Students first develop assessment portfolios that demonstrate their knowledge of, and ability to apply, state teaching standards in their practicum experience. The purpose of these portfolios at the outset is to facilitate and chart their development. In the context of the college course, the portfolios are required, but not graded. Students are counseled as to the future potential value and use of these portfolios as a tool in job seeking. At the end of the credential program, graduates often adapt their portfolios to this second purpose—which is evaluative—as an aid in interviewing for their first teaching positions. Later, as first-year teachers, they use these portfolios for a third purpose—to facilitate and chart their development—this time with their mentors. The portfolios serve as a foundation and directional tool to inform and individualize their continuing professional development. Their portfolios become vehicles for ongoing professional conversation.

Understanding purpose is central to understanding the portfolio. Purpose dictates the type of portfolio to be developed and, by association, indicates both context and audience. In the next section, we discuss purpose in relation to type, context, and audience.

Relationships: Purpose, Type, Context, Structure, and Audience

In this section we discuss how all of these aspects of portfolio orientation— purpose, type, context, structure, and audience—fit together, using purpose as the organizing element. We identify the type, context, structure, and audience most commonly associated with each purpose. Table 3.1 provides an overview of portfolio orientation.

Purpose as it Applies to All Types of Portfolios

Portfolios offer windows into the learning process and, in this way, serve a descriptive function. For many students, the emphasis of previous schooling was on acquiring knowledge, and on the knowledge itself. Little attention was paid to *how* a particular student learns, and how her value system and life experience influence *what* she learns. More recently, individuals' learning styles, strengths, challenges, and ways of knowing have been viewed as important factors in the learning process. Portfolios, in general, function as an

Table 3.1 Portfolio Orientation Overview

Purpose	Type	Context	Structure	Audience
Facilitates and charts development	Developmental	Professional development relationships	Usually single focus; iterative Mentor/mentee	Mentor, self work
Provides a basis for evaluation	Assessment	Preservice teacher preparation Teacher evaluation (of those already practicing) Applying for national teacher certification	Mirrors scope and sequence of standards or criteria	Instructors, certification board
	Professional	Job searches Preparation for promotion	Mirrors requirements and expectations for intended audience	Potential or current employers
Highlights performance and capabilities	Showcase	Professional gatherings Exhibitions	Individualistic; reflects standards or criteria,	Self, instructors, professional community

excellent medium for examining and understanding one's process of growth and development, learning, and change. They provide valuable insights into how and what one learns, and they facilitate that learning.

Portfolios are intended to catalyze self-examination and transformation. They are personal explorations. By way of transformation, this portfolio type is intended to introduce the portfolio builders, or bring them, to a higher level of mindful practice. Langer (1997) describes this notion of mindfulness as having three characteristics: "the continuous creation of new categories; openness to new information, and an implicit awareness of more than one perspective" (p. 4). Mindfulness requires that you bring your habitual ways of doing into consciousness, and then closely examine them in light of new information and fresh perspectives. A portfolio acts, in part, as a journal in which you record and consider connections made between theory and practice.

Purpose 1: To Facilitate and Chart Development

Portfolios in which the primary purpose is to facilitate and chart development emphasize work in progress. They foster the development of knowledge, skills, and dispositions that will be employed in subsequent learning and practice contexts. These portfolios provide a mechanism for increasing self-assessment, reflection, observation, and other skills necessary for reflective professional practice. The builder is not alone in these endeavors. Mentors play an indispensable role—that of engaging the builders in collegial dialogue through which questions are raised, problems are explored, skills are refined, solutions are tested, results are examined, and emotions are expressed.

Developmental Portfolios Facilitate and Chart Development

The *type* of portfolio that facilitates and charts development is called *developmental*. Developmental portfolios are also called "learning" (Wolf & Dietz, 1998) and "professional development" (Dietz, 1995) portfolios. Developmental portfolios function as a means for documenting and charting growth in knowledge, skills, and dispositions over a specified period of time. The "specified period of time" can vary greatly. It can span an accelerated one-month course, a semester course, or a program. By their very nature, developmental portfolios provide a great deal of flexibility. Because they focus on the learning needs of the students, they can be individualized. The instructor or mentor determines their contents, often in dialogue with the student.

At our university, undergraduates in a degree completion option produce developmental portfolios at various points throughout the four semesters of the program. These portfolios document the learner's growing ability to formulate increasingly insightful and pertinent questions and master needed skills. They show progression in the organization of one's thinking and in its complexity. And they demonstrate gains in one's facility in identifying, locating, retrieving, organizing, and presenting data, and identifying and translating conceptual knowledge into practical applications.

Developmental portfolios give the builder room to acquire new knowledge, experiment, practice, analyze, and reflect on real-world tasks that have personal meaning. Successive drafts or reviews of tasks that show increasing understanding or proficiency over time are common to these portfolios. This content reflects the formative nature of developmental portfolios, wherein the builder and mentor systematically analyze progress and identify next steps toward a goal. Developmental portfolios focus on process and self-improvement.

Contexts in Which Developmental Portfolios Are Used

Developmental portfolios are commonly used in contexts in which the participants engage in dialogue meant to broaden and deepen understanding, and to stimulate reflection on practice. These contexts are generally geared toward engaging students in the practical application of knowledge and skills. Bartell and colleagues (1998) describe portfolios as providing a basis for collegial conversations "with a mentor, colleague, or 'critical friend'" (p. 131).

In our work, we use developmental portfolios with two different groups. With final student teachers in a credential program, the portfolio focus is on making connections between standards and students' experiences in field placements. The portfolio gives the student a place to try on reflective habits of mind, apply skills, and examine practice. With practitioners in the degree completion program, the portfolio focus is on using knowledge in new ways, building specific skills and critical self-awareness, and informing ongoing practice. These practitioners often work with one another collaboratively as colleagues, sharing their ideas and drafts, with the goal of helping each other improve, and thus strengthening the work of all. Their efforts are reciprocal and mutually beneficial, and are guided by their mentor. Their mentor helps them establish appropriate benchmarks and timelines, and together they critique and improve portfolio entry ideas, plans, and finished products.

Structure of Developmental Portfolios

Developmental portfolios may be bounded by a brief span of time such as a semester or quarter, and have a single focus. That is, they contain work that is similar in nature. For instance, they may contain iterations of observations and analyses, the point of which is to show students' progress in producing increasingly rich description and thorough, evidence-based analysis. The structure, in this case, might dictate inclusion of all work samples with latest examples first, plus a narrative in which the student summarizes her progress.

Audiences for the Developmental Portfolio

Audiences commonly associated with developmental portfolios include the self, instructors, mentors, and colleagues-as-mentors. Mentors expect and look for evidence of the portfolio builder's growth in several key areas. These include the following: self-assessment of knowledge, skills, and learning needs ("What do I know?"); inquiry ("What else do I need to know and how can I come to know it?"); reflection ("How do I know what I know and what does it all mean?"); and self-assessment of performance and professionalism ("How am I doing?").

Purpose 2: To Provide a Basis for Evaluation

Portfolios used for evaluation purposes provide a basis for judgment of one's performance and accomplishments against established external criteria. They document, for instance, the degree to which a student meets criteria in a course or program. A certain level of success is required before the student can continue in the program or graduate from it. The portfolio reflects the external criteria that are applied. The criteria are based on the standards one must address, such as those developed by the instructor or dictated by the institution, state, or professional association. Evaluation occurs to determine if, and the degree to which, the criteria have been satisfied.

The portfolio also serves as a threshold to future work. It demonstrates one's preparedness to assume positions beyond one's teacher preparation program or current job. The competencies in knowledge, skills, dispositions, and the accomplishments presented provide strong indications of what a school principal or other employer can expect in a candidate's future performance in relation to job expectations. Not only, then, do evaluation portfolios represent the degree to which external criteria have been met, but they also indicate whether given criteria are likely to be met in the future.

Assessment and Professional Portfolios Provide a Basis for Evaluation

Unlike the builder of the developmental portfolio, the builder of an evaluation portfolio does not influence the makeup of the standards, nor does she necessarily influence the performance criteria. These stand outside of the builder. There are two types of portfolios used for evaluation purposes: *assessment* and *professional*.

Assessment portfolios have been part of professional schools (e.g., graphic design, architecture) for a very long time. Schools of education across the country and abroad have adopted portfolios, which are now widely used as tools to assess students' knowledge, skills, dispositions, and accomplishments against state, national, and professional association standards. They are also increasingly being used to assess teacher education programs by bodies such as the National Council for Accreditation of Teacher Education (NCATE). Assessment portfolios provide evidence of what students have learned in relation to specific external criteria, how they know what they know, and how they are able to apply what they know to achieve identified outcomes.

Professional portfolios are a second type used for evaluation purposes. They demonstrate one's potential fit and qualifications relative to employment or promotion criteria within a particular setting. They are tailored to emphasize the best of what one has to offer. They provide a point-in-time portrait of one's knowledge, skills, and dispositions, and they demonstrate the competence with which one can engage these in the work environment. They illuminate, through one's accomplishments, the benefits that the employer would gain by employing or advancing the candidate. Professional portfolios are also called "employment" (Wolf & Dietz, 1998) and "presentation" (Dietz, 1995) portfolios. Professional portfolios are increasingly used in the early care and education field as job-seeking and career advancement tools.

Contexts in Which Evaluation Portfolios Are Used

The most common contexts in which evaluation portfolios are used are in courses or programs and in employment settings. These portfolios include samples of one's best work from which others can determine how well the portfolio builder's skills, knowledge, and dispositions demonstrate competency, or fit the job qualifications, promotion criteria, or certification requirements. The preservice student asks, "How can I demonstrate my competence and readiness to assume a professional position?" The preemployment candidate asks, "How can I use what I've learned to meet the qualifications of this position?" The promotion candidate asks, "How can I prove my readiness to assume greater responsibilities?"

The following examples illustrate how we use these two types of evaluation portfolios. In the culminating experience for child development majors at our university, students complete an assessment portfolio. It is a comprehensive course portfolio in which they document their knowledge of child growth and development in infants, toddlers, and preschoolers using a variety of methods and theoretical frameworks. They demonstrate their skills in observation and analysis, curriculum planning and implementation, and assessment. They reveal their dispositions and growth through ongoing reflection. Through these assessment portfolios, students demonstrate their mastery in areas prescribed in a specific set of guidelines. Students show what they know and what they can do against the backdrop of expectations for knowledge and performance.

This second example of evaluation types illustrates one use of the professional portfolio. The teacher candidate, now a graduate of a teacher preparation program, brings her portfolio to her job interview with the principal of the school in which she would like to work. The principal asks her to describe how she will teach reading to second-graders. As she answers, she opens her portfolio to the curriculum section in which she has displayed photographs with captions detailing real in-classroom experiences with teaching reading. She uses the portfolio as a visual aid that makes her narrative come alive.

Structure for Evaluation Portfolios

The structure of evaluation portfolios is dictated by external criteria. Assessment portfolios are associated with course, program, or accreditation standards or criteria. The structure of the portfolio often mirrors the scope and sequence of the standards or criteria. For instance, assessment portfolios built by students in the teacher education program at our university follow the scope and sequence of the California State Standards for Teachers. Each of six standards must be addressed; each element of each standard must be represented. The portfolios are arranged so that the students' work follows the order in which the standards and elements appear in the state document. This allows the reviewer to progress through the document in logical and predictable order.

Professional portfolios are structured to suit the needs and interests of the intended audience. If, for instance, the portfolio is built in response to an employment vacancy, then the portfolio will reflect the information that the prospective employer has requested, and generally, in the order in which it has been requested. A portfolio built for promotion purposes would include all information required in guidelines the candidate might receive. The order in which the information is presented is no less important for evaluation portfolios than for any other portfolio type. The purpose is to provide all information in a way that will make sense to the reader, and this means providing the information in a way that meets the reader's expectations (follows his or her guidelines).

Audiences for Evaluation Portfolios: Assessment and Professional

Audiences commonly associated with assessment portfolios include instructors, field placement supervisors, and certification boards, such as the National Board for Professional Teaching Standards (NBPTS). For professional portfolios, audiences typically include potential employers and current employers. They may also include scholarship committees, internship evaluators, or admissions boards or committees.

These types of audiences look for and expect to see evidence of excellence and promise. Their evaluations often involve high stakes, since they result in determinations whether or not an individual passes the course, graduates from the program, or secures the job or promotion. They are also frequently competitive, wherein an individual is ranked in relation to others, or is compared against others vying for the same position.

Purpose 3: To Highlight Performance and Capabilities

Portfolios whose purpose is to highlight the builders' performance and capabilities function differently than do all of the other types. They do not serve the same type of summative evaluation purpose as assessment or professional portfolios; they go far beyond the instructive purpose of developmental portfolios. Their focus, instead, is on showcasing builders' accomplishments, and highlighting professional capabilities and interests. Showcasing provides builders with an opportunity to advertise their know-how.

Showcase Portfolios Highlight Performance and Capabilities

The type of portfolio that highlights performance and capabilities is called the *showcase* portfolio. Builders use showcase portfolios as a medium through which they integrate and synthesize their learning to produce complex work products. Rather than demonstrating competence in a variety of discrete elements within a set of standards, as in assessment portfolios, builders of showcase portfolios articulate their learning through products of their design that simultaneously draw on and address multiple standards. The products are made public through their use in the builders' work settings, giving these portfolios an in-the-present, active orientation. They document major learning achieved across the curriculum and provide evidence of integration and application of new knowledge and enhanced skills that are shown to have improved the builders' current practice. These portfolios make available to colleagues in the wider professional community results of important work that the builders have done to improve the quality of existing early care and education programs. They answer the questions, "What am I doing in my current practice?", "How have I used what I've learned in this course or program to improve my practice?", "How am I sharing my work with others?", "What do I have to offer the field?"

Contexts in Which Showcase Portfolios Are Used

Showcase portfolios are primarily used in the contexts of exhibitions or presentations to a professional community. They may be used in settings where employers come to shop for prospective employees. We use this type of portfolio in the child development degree completion option at our university. At their exhibition celebration, program graduates display their showcase portfolios, which highlight their learning and accomplishments as evidenced by specific work products. They share these accomplishments and products with their peers, instructors, families, and with the larger early care and education community. In this context, showcase portfolios aid graduates, who are working professionals, and the program in achieving four goals:

1. to contribute to and foster best practice,
2. to engage in and promote reflective practice, collaboration, and lifelong learning,
3. to cultivate a professional culture that thrives on inquiry and dialogue, and
4. to provide leadership in the early care and education field.

Structure for Showcase Portfolios

Showcase portfolios can be highly individualistic. Nonetheless, guidelines or standards are often involved. Attending to the scope and sequence requirements delineated in the course or program is essential, just as it is for all other portfolio types. Showcase portfolios document progress and competency through the presentation of selected samples that show best work across the criteria. Structure may vary widely. It can follow the standards, as in the example under assessment portfolios. Or, as in the showcase examples we share in this book (see Chapter 6), students present their work in the form of projects, that cumulatively document mastery in all standards. The portfolio is structured by project, rather than by standard.

Audiences for Showcase Portfolios

Audiences commonly associated with showcase portfolios include instructors, colleagues in the wider professional community, peers, family members, prospective employers, and others connected in official capacities with the program, such as deans and department heads. Like the audiences for evaluation portfolios, showcase audiences are looking for and expect to see evidence of excellence. They also, however, anticipate innovation—new ways of addressing old problems and fresh expressions of recurring themes.

A Final Note

Understanding purpose, type, context, structure, and audience and their interaction is an important step in preparing to undertake the development of a portfolio. Having a clear orientation, led by certain knowledge of your portfolio's purpose, sets the direction for all of the work that follows.

four
Planning and Organizing for a Successful Portfolio

Planning is bringing the future into the present so that you can do something about it now.

—Alan Lakein

Readers who are developing *assessment* or *showcase* portfolios as part of college or university classes or programs will find this chapter especially relevant. Planning and organizing are necessary and advisable for every portfolio type; assessment and showcase portfolios demand a disciplined and systematic approach. This chapter is essential to those whose portfolios will be used to assess particular competencies or showcase their strengths and accomplishments in an integrated way. However, we expect that those who are building developmental or professional portfolios will find the information useful as well.

Building a portfolio, like any large undertaking, can seem daunting at first. And as happens quite often when confronted with a new project or problem, it is tempting to just dive right in. Working on the fly can be a habit—a way of working—figuring things out along the way and hoping it all comes out right in the end. All too often though, this approach leads to trouble or unwanted outcomes. The task can take more time than expected, result in parts that need to be redone, or leave you with a job completed, but not to your satisfaction. Sometimes, it leads to failure or unrealized goals and those nagging regrets, "I wish I'd thought of that before . . .," or "If only I had. . . ." As businessman Sir John Harvey-Jones once said, "Planning is an unnatural process; it is much more fun to do something. The nicest thing about not planning is that failure comes as a complete surprise."

Consider this often-heard conversation.

Professor: Have you planned out what you're going to do?
Student: We don't have time to plan, we have to get started.
Professor: Where are you going to start? Have you figured out who's going to do what and how much time things will take?
Student: We don't know yet. There's a bunch of stuff we need to do. It all has to get done. We'll figure it out once we get started. We're just gonna jump in.

An unplanned, disorganized approach is almost guaranteed to lead to a project trajectory that is conveyed by Figure 4.1.

What, then, are the antidotes to the *"complete surprise"* noted by Harvey-Jones? PLANNING and ORGANIZATION! This chapter serves as a reminder that bringing any size project to fruition is a process, one that requires forethought and preparation. An important part of the process is careful, realistic planning—the most underappreciated and overlooked activity—and organizing: making information easier to retrieve, synthesize, work with, and convey. Planning and organizing can seem as intimidating as building the portfolio itself. But they need not be. The purpose of this chapter is to help you avoid less than desirable consequences and, instead, make sure and

FIGURE 4.1 I'm Lost!

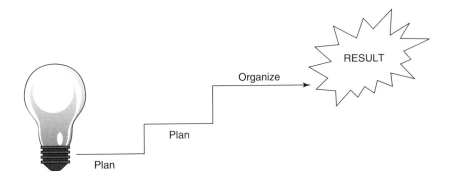

FIGURE 4.2 Sure and Steady Progress

steady progress toward the high quality result you want. We present some tools that can help smooth the way.

Excellent outcomes are not accidental or the result of haphazard or chaotic activity. They come about, in large part, due to the time we dedicate and activities we undertake to help us think through and map out how to get from a promising idea to a successful result. There are two aspects that come into play here; both indispensable to the effort: Planning and Organizing. To give each aspect its full measure, we have divided this chapter into a section on each. We start with planning.

Planning Overview

Planning is a thinking process—the "intentional pause" or "goal-directed mental space" *we purposely create* between an idea and its implementation. It requires a global perspective on the work to be completed—a clear view of the big picture, goal, or outcome. "Global perspective" also implies having a good idea of what the final product will look like. Planning applies to every component of a portfolio, such as a lesson plan, a unit, or a project, as well as to the portfolio in its entirety.

Having a firm grasp of the expectations you need to meet is the best place to start the planning process. Expectations spring from the *type of portfolio* you will develop, the *standards* you will be striving to meet, the *specific structure* required, and the *span of time* over which you will develop the portfolio. Once you know the type of portfolio you will create and its purpose, becoming familiar with the standards to which you will be held—to the extent that you have them firmly in mind—will be of enormous help as you proceed through the planning and data collection/development processes.

We have provided two different scenarios to illustrate how *portfolio type*, *structure*, *standards*, and *time frame* drive the planning process (and reflect the final result). These two scenarios also illustrate how open-ended or tightly structured portfolios can be based on the purpose they serve.

Scenario 1 relates to students in the Child Development Practitioner Option who have returned to college to complete their undergraduate degrees in Child Development. They are already professionals in the early care and education (ECE) field, having worked anywhere from three to 43 years with young children. These students are given a great deal of autonomy in determining the content and themes of their portfolio entries due to their standing as practicing professionals and their specific work-related interests and needs. Their portfolios consist of a set of comprehensive projects that reflect the type of ECE setting in which they work, the age groups in their settings, and their individual positions in their programs.

In Scenario 1, students are required to build a **showcase portfolio** (*type*) that demonstrates, through a **series of projects** (*organizational structure*), what they know and are able to do that reflect the competencies identified in the **NAEYC Standards for Programs** (*standards*). The portfolio is a record of their acquisition of new knowledge and their adaptation of that knowledge to novel situations over a **two-year period**—the span of their program (*time frame*). Notice that expectations are clear with regard to *type, organizational structure, standards*, and *time frame* as shown in Table 4.1.

In Scenario 2, pre-service elementary education teachers build an assessment portfolio that includes, for instance, the Integrated Curriculum Unit. The portfolio is based on the California Standards for the Teaching Profession. These students are enrolled in a teacher education credential program with a focus on kindergarten through third grade. However, in order to meet state requirements for their teaching credential, the program includes an upper grade reading class and practicum experience in the first semester. The students build an **assessment portfolio** (*type*) based on the **California Standards for the Teaching Profession** (*standards*). These **six standards** each have up to **seven elements** (*organizational structure*). Students build their portfolios over a period of **three semesters** (*time frame*). Expectations for this portfolio are shown in Table 4.2.

Scenario 1: Showcase Portfolio

Planning, in the Scenario 1 example, begins with understanding the purpose of a showcase portfolio:

> To highlight performance and capabilities through the production of complex work products. Showcase portfolios document major learning across the curriculum and provide evidence of integration, application, and adaptation of new knowledge and enhanced skills that are shown to have improved the builders' current practice.

Table 4.1 Factors that Drive Planning: Scenario 1

Portfolio type	*Showcase*
Structure	*Series of projects*
Standards	*NAEYC Standards for Programs*
Time frame	*Two-year period*

Table 4.2 Factors that Drive Planning: Scenario 2

Portfolio type	*Assessment*
Structure	*Standards/elements*
Standards	*California Standards for the Teaching Profession*
Time frame	*Three-semester period*

As with all portfolio types, showcase portfolios can comprise a wide variety of sections and headings. Sections and headings will reflect the unique characteristics and requirements of the document you produce. In this example, the portfolio features several overarching pieces: a self-introduction, philosophy statement, and global reflection, in addition to four content-specific projects that are documented through in-depth evidence and accompanied by focused reflections. Figure 4.3 provides an overview of the portfolio example we provide here. A graphic representation like this can be extremely useful to the portfolio builder because it provides the global picture of the finished product. In the event that a graphic representation has not been provided for you, it can be very helpful to develop one yourself.

Once you have a clear picture of the whole, and how the parts relate to each other and to the whole, you can explore the criteria in more detail and their relationship to the standards for your particular portfolio.

Criteria for Projects

Criteria for your portfolio will be unique to your circumstances. Keep in mind that the criteria shown here represent only one example of what is possible, and are offered to give you an idea of how criteria guide portfolio content. The criteria for projects in this example include the following:

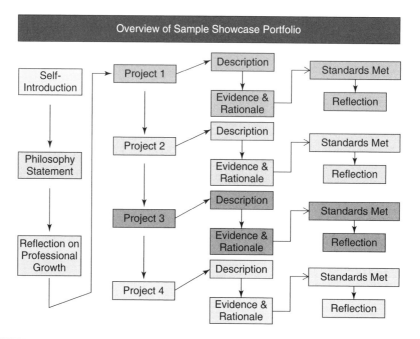

FIGURE 4.3 Overview of Sample Showcase Portfolio

- Projects must be original. Students devise projects that both reflect course content and, at the same time, address a felt or expressed need in their work setting.
- Each required project corresponds to a specific content area. Content areas include child development, play, and learning; curriculum; working with families; and advocacy or program evaluation. All content areas must be represented by a project.
- Each project must be multidimensional, meeting at least two standards, with all standards addressed across the four projects.
- Each project must be evaluated by end users; the results of the evaluation become part of the finished project. For instance, if a project is one in which a professional development program is offered to local family child care association members, then the attendees must evaluate the outcome.
- Each project must be accompanied by a rationale statement. The rationale statement must:

   o Identify each artifact included in the portfolio for each project
   o Provide an analysis of the essential elements of the artifact/s
   o Include your argument for the artifact/s based on professional knowledge (draw on professional literature and personal practical knowledge)
   o Explain how the artifact/s demonstrate/s competency in corresponding standards
   o Explain what the artifact/s say about your understanding of child development and the standards.

   (Adapted from University of Florida course handout)

See Chapter 7 for more on writing rationale statements.

Project Planning Tools

We present a set of questions that we use to guide students through every step of planning a project, leaving nothing to chance. The questions help focus thinking, make learning explicit, and develop a roadmap that will guide the student to a successful result. The questions can be helpful whether you are planning a project, a unit, a lesson plan, or any other type of complex portfolio entry. We invite you to tailor the questions to your specific portfolio planning needs.

The worksheet shown in Table 4.3 is provided to students when they first start to think about a project they want to do to meet requirements in a particular content area. For our purposes here, we have provided a sample response to each question to demonstrate how the questions focus thinking through a project. We also note where in the planning process, and in what

Table 4.3 Thinking through Your Project: A Portfolio Planning Worksheet

Name _____   Project # _____

THINKING THROUGH YOUR PROJECT

A Portfolio Planning Worksheet

On separate sheets of paper or in a notebook, answer each of the questions below in as much detail as possible in preparation for your project.

1. **Major learning achieved:** What are some of the big ideas you've taken away from this course/program that have influenced or made you examine your practice?

2. **Identify audiences with which to share your knowledge.** To whom, besides yourself, would this knowledge be useful and why?

3. **Which of the big ideas you identified in #1 are best suited to a multidimensional project?** What applications or projects do they suggest?

4. **Outline a project idea that best expresses the big ideas you identified in #3 and will allow you to convey what you've learned to an appropriate audience.** What will your project accomplish, provide, or result in? Describe your project as clearly and concisely as you can. Who is your audience? What are your goals? Make sure they are achievable.

5. **Sum up in a few words the project you plan to do.**

6. **What tangible product/s will result from your project?** For instance, the product may be a service you provide, materials you develop, curriculum you plan and implement.

7. **What evidence will you produce to document your project?** Your documentation should be such that it would allow someone else to duplicate the project if they chose to do so.

8. **Who will benefit from your project and how?** Who is your audience and what do you want them to take away from your project? Don't forget to include yourself as a beneficiary.

9. **Will you have partners in your project?** Who will they be? How will you engage them? What part will they have in the project? How will tasks be divided and managed? Who will lead the project?

10. **What is your timeline?** When will you start each step? How long will each step take? When will you implement your project?

11. **Is the project likely to cost money?** How much and for what? Are funds available? From where?

12. **How will you evaluate your project?** Does your evaluation require you to develop an instrument? If so, what? Will you need the help of others to administer the instrument? If so, who, and how will you include them?

13. **Which standards do you anticipate your project meeting and how?** Be specific in how each will be met. As with all parts of the planning process, you are looking ahead.

14. **What obstacles might you encounter?** How will you avoid, minimize, or address them?

ways, reflection is needed. Bear in mind that not every project you undertake will require an answer to every question. However, considering each question in relation to your project can aid you in thinking things through in a systematic and comprehensive manner. A primary purpose of planning is to avoid unnecessary delays and disappointments later.

The sample responses address a content area called "Child Development, Play, and Learning." The numbered questions appear on the worksheet; the italicized text below each number represents a student's responses for the project being planned.

Sample Responses to Worksheet Questions that Guide Thinking through a Project

1. **Major learning achieved:** What are some of the big ideas you've taken away from this course/program that have influenced or made you examine your practice?
   Note: This is an important point of reflection in your planning process! Think back on your learning. Why do these particular ideas resonate with you?

   a. *With the emphasis on academics with younger and younger children, teachers and parents need to be reminded or educated about how important play is to children's learning and social-emotional development.*
   b. *Play means different things and looks differently in different cultural groups.*
   c. *High quality play doesn't happen by accident. It requires adequate, uninterrupted time, observation and planning, and facilitation and support.*
   d. *Play is meaningful to children and facilitates learning and development in all of the domains.*
   e. *Often times, "behavior problems" boil down to children not having good play skills or not knowing how to enter play successfully. These can be taught!*

   Reflection: Parents often pressure me to add more academics to my program and stress kindergarten readiness as the reason. I get frustrated because academics for 3-year-olds is not developmentally appropriate, but I realize that I don't know how to explain this to parents effectively.

2. **Identify audiences with which to share your knowledge.** To whom, besides yourself, would this knowledge be useful and why?
   This will be useful to staff in my program because it will help them plan curriculum that is developmentally appropriate. It will also be useful for

parents because it will help them understand why play is important and how it contributes to learning and school success.

3. **Which of the big ideas you identified in #1 are best suited to a multidimensional project?** What applications or projects do they suggest?
   A, B, and D. They suggest some kind of educational event for parents that focuses on the benefits of play and how play helps prepare children for kindergarten.

4. **Outline a project idea that best expresses the big ideas you identified in #3 and will allow you to convey what you've learned to an appropriate audience.** What will your project accomplish, provide, or result in? Describe your project as clearly and concisely as you can. Who is your audience? What are your goals? Make sure they are achievable.
   Family Day is an event to bring parents and staff at our center together to play and learn. It has 3 purposes: to build a stronger sense of community among families at the center, to educate parents about play—its benefits, what good play looks like, and why it's important and meaningful for their children, and to encourage parent involvement.

5. **Sum up in a few words the project you plan to do.**
   Family Play Day at the Center.

6. **What tangible product/s will result from your project?** For instance, the product may be a service you provide, materials you develop, curriculum you plan and implement.
   We will produce 2 products for parents: 1) samples of the children's work that each have a description attached to that tells parents how the activity contributes to kindergarten readiness; and 2) a handout of simple, low or no-cost learning activities, crafts, and experiments that parents can do with their children at home.

7. **What evidence will you produce to document your project?** Your documentation should be such that it would allow someone else to duplicate the project if they chose to do so.

   ○ *event flyer in English and Spanish announcing the event and the letter that we send home with the children*
   ○ *photos of the event*
   ○ *handouts we give to parents on simple games they can play with their children*
   ○ *samples of children's work with the note to parents about their learning*
   ○ *the sign-up sheets we use for parent involvement*
   ○ *a summary of the evaluations of the event*

○ *notes from planning meetings*
○ *displays that explain children's play*
○ *the questionnaire we give to parents.*

8. **Who will benefit from your project and how?** Who is your audience and what do you want them to take away from your project? Don't forget to include yourself as a beneficiary.

○ *Parents will benefit by being with or making friends, learning more about the center and how we help their children succeed, learning how play helps children prepare for kindergarten, and seeing opportunities to be involved in the program.*
○ *The center benefits by helping parents be more effective partners in their children's education and by strengthening the relationships between staff and parents.*
○ *By sharing my knowledge with others, I help improve my center, and become a more qualified professional.*

9. **Will you have partners in your project?** Who will they be? How will you engage them? What part will they have in the project? How will tasks be divided and managed? Who will lead the project?
The staff and director will be my partners. To engage them, I'll present the idea in detail, including who it will benefit and how, and ask for their help in planning and implementing the event. I will manage the event planning.

10. **What is your timeline?** When will you start each step? How long will each step take? When will you implement your project?
February 15–28: Get permission from my director to have the event and get the staff on board. Invite parents and staff to help on project and form a planning committee.
March 10: First planning meeting:

○ *Decide on a day and time for the event*
○ *Decide what activities would help us achieve each purpose*
○ *Decide who will do what, whether we need more people to help and how many. Start making contacts. Form committees*
○ *Write a brief, but detailed description of the event to use when approaching groups for help.*

March 11–31: Contact groups to provide refreshments, information, donations. Start collecting children's work samples, start working on explanations of children's work that will be attached.

April 1–30: Confirm participation by groups. Start working on summer activity handouts, develop flyer and letter to parents, start making/collecting decorations.
May 1: Go over all preparations and check that everything has been covered.
May 2–4: Make all last minute preparations.
May 15: The Event.

11. **Is the project likely to cost money?** How much and for what? Are funds available? From where?
    Budget: If 50 families attend the event, that's about 65 children under 6 and 30 children from 6–12.

Flyers, letters, handouts	*$10.00*
Decorations	*$50.00*
Paper goods for refreshments	*$20.00*
Miscellaneous	*$10.00*
Total	*$90.00*

I'll ask the director if we can use money from the center's publicity fund for the event.

12. **How will you evaluate your project?** Does your evaluation require you to develop an instrument? If so, what? Will you need the help of others to administer the instrument? If so, who, and how will you include them?
    We will ask parents to complete a follow-up questionnaire that we will design. We will offer a light snack when they come to pick up their children on the Monday after the event and ask them to fill it out then. The staff will help design the questionnaire.

13. **Which standards do you anticipate your project meeting and how?** Be specific in how each will be met. As with all parts of the planning process, you are looking ahead.
    My project will meet the following NAEYC standards:
    Standard 2. Building Family and Community Relationships
    Students prepared in early childhood degree programs understand that successful early childhood education depends upon partnerships with children's families and communities. They know about, understand, and value the importance and complex characteristics of children's families and communities. They use this understanding to create respectful, reciprocal relationships that support and empower families and to involve all families in their children's development and learning.

○   *2b: Supporting and engaging families and communities through respectful, reciprocal relationships*
○   *2c: Involving families and communities in their children's development and learning.*

Family Day celebrates families and shows parents that we value them and want them to be an integral part of our school. We know that not every parent can spend time in the classroom, so we have given parents as many ideas as possible for how they can be involved. The information we give parents with their children's work helps them understand growth and development and the activity ideas helps empower them to help their children prepare for kindergarten.

Standard 4. Using Developmentally Effective Approaches to Connect with Children and Families

Students prepared in early childhood degree programs understand that teaching and learning with young children is a complex enterprise, and its details vary depending on children's ages, characteristics, and the settings within which teaching and learning occur. They understand and use positive relationships and supportive interactions as the foundation for their work with young children and families. Students know, understand, and use a wide array of developmentally appropriate approaches, instructional strategies, and tools to connect with children and families and positively influence each child's development and learning.

○   *Sub-Standard 4a: Understanding positive relationships and supportive interactions as the foundation of their work with children*

We know children do better in school when parents and teachers are partners in their education. We are trying to cement this partnership early in their children's schooling.

○   *Sub-Standard 4b: Knowing and understanding effective strategies and tools for early education*

The children's work represents projects the children have done in science, art, social studies, and dramatic play. In each case, the work has been developmentally appropriate and has followed interests that the children have expressed. Our display of their work points this out to parents and we talk with them about it when they view the display.

Note: The conclusion of the project marks an important point of reflection with regard to standards. You will want to reflect on which standards the project <u>actually</u> met and how it met them. Revise as needed from your initial educated guess. Be sure to use examples from the project to illustrate your points.

14. **What obstacles might you encounter?** How will you avoid, minimize, or address them?

 ○ *The teachers or director might resist the idea. I have to present a clear vision of the event, how much time it will take, and who will benefit and how. If they still don't want to do it, I'll scale it back and do it for my classroom.*
 ○ *All or part of the funds may not be available. Scale the event to fit available funds. Hold a bake sale and garage sale to collect funds.*

Figure 4.4 provides a graphic view of the portfolio project planning process described above. It shows how students move from course content to identifying big ideas to gradually translating ideas into tangible projects that can be implemented, evaluated, and connected to standards.

Reflecting on the Project

As we have stated elsewhere, human beings convert experience into personal knowledge through reflection. As with all aspects of portfolio development, reflection plays a part in the planning process. There are several points in the process where reflection is a factor, as shown by the "Notes" in the list of questions above (#s 1 and 13). The first point of reflection is in "Major Learning" (#1). The time you take to think about why some knowledge has

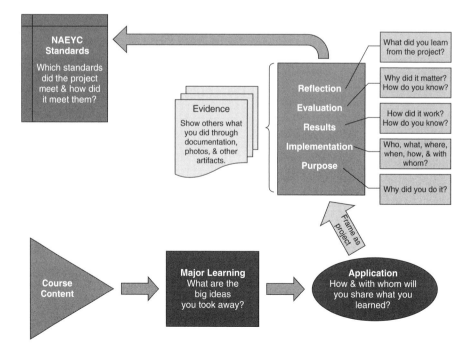

FIGURE 4.4 Portfolio Project Planning Process

made a significant impact on you and has affected your thinking in a particular way can give you important insights. This metacognition (thinking about thinking) can tap beliefs or ideas of which you have been unaware or to which have not given a great deal of thought. The awareness that comes of the reflection can aid you in tackling an issue in a new way or gaining understanding that informs and molds your practice.

Another important point of reflection, both as you plan and after you complete the project, comes in Standards you anticipate meeting (#13). The quality of the reflection you achieve here is dependent upon your fully understanding each standard and being able to think about its implications as you apply it in the real world. How have you translated the standard into meaningful action?

Scenario 2: Assessment Portfolio

Whereas in Scenario 1, where the students have a great deal of autonomy, the choices students in Scenario 2 have are much more limited. For instance, when it comes time to select a topic for developing a teaching unit, the students are restricted to specific requirements from their curriculum instructor (science, social studies, and language arts), in combination with the latitude offered by their classroom teacher. For instance, in the fall semester, students might have a wide choice of topics from which to choose, whereas in the spring, choices are limited by what has already been taught.

Planning in Scenario 2 begins with understanding the purpose of the assessment portfolio:

> To provide a basis for judgment of one's performance and accomplishments against established external criteria and the degree to which a student meets criteria in a course or program. Assessment portfolios provide evidence of what students have learned in relation to specific external criteria, how they know what they know, and how they are able to apply what they know to achieve identified outcomes.

Portfolio Planning Tools

Two electronic formats are highly useful in planning portfolio development. The first is the spreadsheet (Hawkins & Black, 2004). The second is a table. In both formats, the standards and all of their elements can be arrayed. However, the spreadsheet is more versatile because of its expandability. Data can be added indefinitely without regard for the page boundaries integral to word processing documents. Regardless of whether students use spreadsheets or tables, these tools help them connect their assignments and experiences to the standards and track their progress. We have provided three variations of spreadsheets or tables that are used by students. These variations are geared for students needing a great deal of detail, some detail, and little detail.

Table 4.4 illustrates how one of the standards and its accompanying six elements are organized in a spreadsheet. This variation provides a great deal of detail. Because of space issues on the printed page, we have displayed a snapshot of Standard 1 from the full spreadsheet which would include all six standards and each of their elements in full detail. Imagine that the spreadsheet continues expanding to the right with the same amount of detail for the other five standards. The scrolling function enables users to move easily across and around the data in a worksheet that can be more than one page wide. This very detailed example, Table 4.4, includes the title of the standard on row 3, and the element numbers and their full descriptions on row 4. This format requires students to match their activities to the corresponding element of a standard. Row 5 shows the information entered by the student that explains the activities she implemented to meet the element. In this example, the initial assignment, a Get Acquainted lesson plan, is used to demonstrate how an activity or experience can meet more than one element of a standard. Note that this lesson plan example also fits with elements in other standards (see Table 4.6).

An alternative to the use of spreadsheets is the use of tables, a feature found in word processing software. Tables allow a user to set up a tabular tracking system that fits on a standard size page. A student who needs less detail can set up her table that includes all of the standards with their full titles on a single page. The elements are not shown (Table 4.5). The student lists her activities and indicates, using key words and element numbers, that she has addressed the element. For example, students plan summative and formative assessments as part of a curriculum unit they design and implement with K-3 students (see shaded boxes in Table 4.5).

As the students become more familiar with the standards and elements, they often switch to using little detail and adopt a system whereby they use only the element numbers (e.g., 1.1) for keeping track of their assignments and experiences (see Table 4.6).

As the students do assignments or projects in their courses, they add them to their spreadsheet file or table and identify how each fits the standards and elements. Over the course of the three semesters, students will have recorded multiple examples for each standard from which to select their best examples for inclusion in their portfolios. Planning entails monitoring the number and quality of examples they have acquired for each standard, determining gaps, and mapping further activity to address the gaps.

Organizing Overview

Organizing implies structuring or arranging things, whatever they might be, into a coherent whole. With regard to portfolios, organizing makes it

Table 4.4 Standard 1 and Get Acquainted Lesson Plan in Spreadsheet File Format, Highest Level of Detail

	A	B	C	D	E	F	G	H
1								
2		California Standards for the Teaching Profession, 2009						
3	Student Assignments			STANDARD 1 ENGAGING AND SUPPORTING ALL STUDENTS IN LEARNING				
4		1.1 Using knowledge of students to engage them in learning	1.2 Connecting learning to students' prior knowledge, backgrounds, life experiences, and interests	1.3 Connecting subject matter to meaningful, real-life contexts	1.4 Using a variety of instructional strategies, resources, and technologies to meet students' diverse learning needs	1.5 Promoting critical thinking through inquiry, problem solving, and reflection	1.6 Monitoring student learning and adjusting instruction while teaching	
5	Get Acquainted lesson plan	Building trust and observing strengths, interests, and needs	Identifying areas of interest which can be included in plans for future lesson plans		Use a variety of activities: ex: Acrostic poem using student's name, game format "getting to know each other" game board, discovering what you have in common			

Table 4.5 Six Standards, Two Student Assignments, Key Words and Element Numbers, Table Format

Student assignments	California Standards for the Teaching Profession, 2009					
	Standard 1 Engaging and Supporting All Students in Learning	Standard 2 Creating and Maintaining Effective Environments for Student Learning	Standard 3 Understanding and Organizing Subject Matter for Student Learning	Standard 4 Planning Instruction and Designing Learning for All Students	Standard 5 Assessing Students for Learning	Standard 6 Developing as a Professional Educator
Integrated Curriculum Unit			Web 3.1, 3.3, 3.4	Specific for students in small group, 4.1, 4.2, 4.3, 4.4, 4.5	**Formative and Pre-post test 5.1, 5.4**	
Reading					Running records 5.1, 5.2, 5.3, 5.4	

Table 4.6 Six Standards and Two Student Assignments with Just Element Numbers Listed, Table Format

Student Assignments	California Standards for the Teaching Profession, 2009					
	Standard 1 Engaging and Supporting All Students in Learning	**Standard 2** Creating and Maintaining Effective Environments for Student Learning	**Standard 3** Understanding and Organizing Subject Matter for Student Learning	**Standard 4** Planning Instruction and Designing Learning for All Students	**Standard 5** Assessing Students for Learning	**Standard 6** Developing as a Professional Educator
Get Acquainted lesson plan	1.1, 1.2					
Sequence of social studies/reading activities	1.1,1.2, 1.3, 1.4, 1.6	2.1, 2.3, 2.5, 2.6, 2.7		4.1, 4.2	5.2	

possible to make sense of the whole and how each part contributes to the whole. It facilitates the identification of gaps, redundancies, and overlap, as well as patterns and trends. Organizing facilitates synthesis and deep reflection, both of which are requisite to the development of new knowledge. And finally, organizing allows you to communicate your efforts and your understanding of your professional capabilities and limitations in a manner that is accessible to others. Organizing brings order where there might otherwise be chaos, or at least disarray!

The Information Literacy Fact Sheet of the California State University Information Competence Project (Dunn, 2000) describes information literacy as "a set of abilities requiring individuals to 'recognize when information is needed and have the ability to locate, evaluate, and use effectively the needed information.'" Although this project focused on identifying skills necessary to navigate the technological advances in the information age, the skills can be more broadly applied to the collection, management, and conveyance of all types of information and materials, technology-based or not. The fact sheet lists skills that are vital to the information literate individual and can be instructive to the portfolio builder (we have made some additions that relate to portfolio development, shown in square brackets). The first two skills apply to *organizing* (shown in bold), so we have explored them in relation to portfolio preparation. The rest of the skills apply to other aspects of building portfolios and are not examined in depth here. Skills of the information literate individual include the following:

- **Determining the extent [and kind] of information needed.**
- **[Collecting, categorizing, and] accessing the needed information effectively and efficiently.**
- Evaluating information and its sources critically.
- Incorporating selected information into one's knowledge base [and justify its inclusion].
- Using information effectively to accomplish a specific purpose.
- Understanding the economic, legal, and social issues surrounding the use of information, and access and use information ethically and legally.

(Adapted from Dunn, October 2, 2000,
California State University Information Literacy Fact Sheet)

Determining the Extent and Kind of Information Needed

Organizing begins at the beginning—with collecting. As you build your portfolio, you will be generating and amassing a great number of artifacts and written materials that correspond to various components of the portfolio. A project, lesson plan, or other activity you develop, and any specific guidelines you may receive will indicate *the extent and kind of information needed*.

For instance, you may be planning and conducting a social studies lesson for fifth graders. Depending upon your specific requirements, you might have a curriculum web, a pre-assessment of students' knowledge of the subject you are going to teach, detailed resource and materials lists, samples of children's work, photos of the experience, children's reflections on their learning, a post-test of children's acquired knowledge, etc. Your initial planning— thinking through preparation for and implementation of your lesson—is the time to anticipate this group of items. It is also the time to develop a storage plan—where and how will they be categorized and stored.

Collecting, Categorizing, and Accessing the Needed Information Effectively and Efficiently

During the development and collection phase, KEEP EVERYTHING. Evaluating will come later. As you create and gather artifacts and other materials, it is critical that you file them in a way that:

- keeps them together,
- categorizes them,
- makes them readily accessible, and
- facilitates later retrieval.

You do not want to find yourself at any point in the process asking, "Now that I've done all this work and have all this stuff, what do I do with it?" Keep a handle on it as you go. Some portfolios span multiple semesters or years, making organizing materials all the more essential. Table 4.4, shown in Scenario 2, is an example of a tool used at the beginning of the portfolio process to keep track of and categorize artifacts as they are being developed and implemented. It is arranged by assignment and standard. Another tool (shown in Table 4.7) is arranged by portfolio component. Notice in the tool shown in Table 4.7 that column 2 is labeled Filename. When you manage information electronically, retrieval depends upon being able to locate where on the hard drive or other storage device you have saved something. Endless frustration comes of not attending to the "where" of electronic storage. Make sure you backup your data *as you go* to avoid another major source of frustration and anxiety expressed by the now famous last words, "My computer crashed. I lost everything!"

Setting up a Storage System

Moving into the organizational phase of the work requires setting up a system for filing artifacts and materials. Filing systems can be physical or electronic, and sometimes include both. The representations we provide as examples translate well for either physical or electronic storage.

Table 4.7 Organizing Tool Arranged by Portfolio Component

Worksheet Organizing Portfolio Components			
PORTFOLIO COMPONENT	FILENAME	WORK COMPLETED/ EVIDENCE ALREADY DEVELOPED OR COLLECTED	WORK/EVIDENCE STILL NEEDED
Self-Introduction (keep notes as you think of things to include)			
Philosophy Statement (file drafts as you write/rewrite them)			
Global Reflection (keep notes as you reflect on your experiences; file copies of reflections you write for various components/ assignments)			
Project 1 (file everything you collect or develop for this project)			
Project 2 (file everything you collect or develop for this project)			
Project 3 (file everything you collect or develop for this project)			
Project 4 (file everything you collect or develop for this project)			

Earlier in this chapter, we discussed the Integrated Curriculum Unit assignment associated with the California Teaching Standards, and the ECE Practitioner portfolio comprised of a set of comprehensive projects. We use these two examples to show how organization of artifacts and materials might look. These illustrations apply equally well to both physical and electronic filing systems.

The file for Standard 3: Understanding and Organizing Subject Matter for Student Learning, shown in Figure 4.5, will include a set of files which house categorized items created or collected over the course of the credential program to demonstrate competence in Standard 3. It may include a unit web, grade level content standards, lesson plans, photos of students doing the work, and pictures of bulletin boards or charts that were used. The file may also contain important contextual information about the class, such as grade level, range of reading levels, special needs, languages spoken, and resources available. In the example of the Practitioner Portfolio, shown in Figure 4.6,

FIGURE 4.5 File Organization for Standard 3

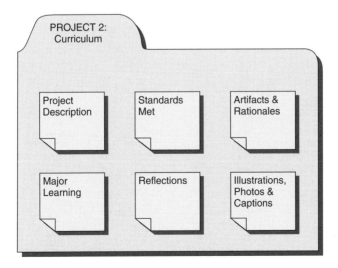

FIGURE 4.6 File organization for Project 2: Curriculum

each project has its own file, as do the other components such as Philosophy and Global Reflection. Files within the file correspond to components required for projects, rather than being arranged by standard.

A Bird's Eye View of an Organization System

Figure 4.7 illustrates what the overall system of organization looks like. Whether physical or electronic storage is used, a container to hold all of the data is necessary. For physical materials, this might be a file cabinet or file box. For electronic materials, it will be a master file on a hard drive or other electronic storage device. The large box shown in Figure 4.7 represents the container. Files within the container represent physical file folders or electronic files. These are labeled and categorized by content. Individual pieces of hard copy evidence or electronic documents are located within content files. When the time arrives for you to assemble your portfolio, you will have everything at hand, arranged in a manner that facilitates fast and easy retrieval.

As we illustrate in Figure 4.7, data (e.g., lesson plan) associated with various portfolio components (e.g., Standard 3) are initially organized into individual files within their own files. As some point, however, all of these separate files will be brought together into the finished product—your portfolio. We offer one last set of graphics to show how this can be accomplished with a minimum of fuss.

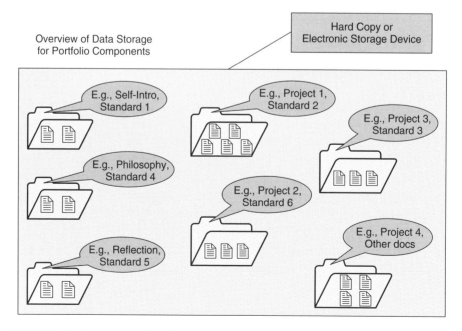

FIGURE 4.7 Overview of Data Storage for Portfolio Components

In Figure 4.8, the large arrows point out the file that holds all documentation pertaining to the portfolio component labeled Project 2, and (sub)files into which the documentation is sorted within that main file. There are a few more steps that will help you go from unconnected pieces to the finished portfolio. In preparation of the final product, all of the components and their parts must be condensed and combined. Creating a new (sub)file for each component suits this purpose. Notice the circled file called Project 2 in Figure 4.8. As you review, sift, sort, arrange, rearrange, and mesh the contents of each (sub)file, you can use the new (sub)file as a place to work up a final draft. Once the draft is complete, it can sit there undisturbed until you are ready for final assembly of the portfolio.

Beyond the Hard Drive: Saving Your Portfolio to a Portable Electronic Storage Device

The rate at which technology moves, as we all know, is staggering. In just a few short decades, we have seen vinyl magnetic tape sound recordings (i.e., vinyl records and audio cassettes) all but disappear. Store shelves are now full of digital recording devices from CDs (compact discs) to DVDs (digital video/versatile discs), to USB flash drives (also called thumb drives or key drives) or memory cards (also called memory sticks) (Griffith, 2010). When you read this, there will likely be something new—we can only imagine!

Any of the digital storage devices listed above make good "containers" for portfolios. Two of their benefits are portability and affordability. From the standpoint of storage capacity, CDs are generally the most limited of

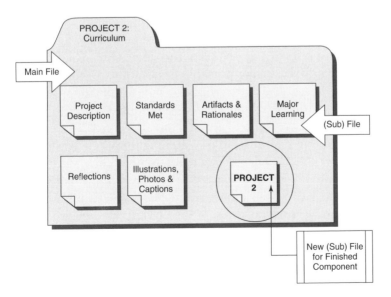

FIGURE 4.8 Consolidating Data for a Portfolio Component

FIGURE 4.9 Bringing the Components of the Portfolio Together into a Finished Product

the choices. Flash drives and memory cards have the most capacity. Capacity becomes an important consideration if your portfolio contains photographs, video clips, audio clips, or graphics, as these take up a lot of digital space.

Typically, students construct their portfolios on the hard drives of their desk top computers or their laptops. That time finally comes, however, when the portfolio has to be saved to a portable storage device for distribution. This is a critical step that requires great care. The portfolio in its entirety must be saved to the portable device. This is why we encourage students to organize their materials as we have outlined in this chapter. If done this way, with the whole portfolio contained within one integrated file, then opying the portfolio to another location (read "storage device") is painless and trouble-free. Instead of searching for a bunch of disconnected files spread over the hard drive, one file is copied. Once the portfolio is in its new home, the final organizing task lays in inserting hyperlinks that will connect documents to each other within the portfolio and to supporting documents outside of the portfolio proper, but in the same master file. This last task, hyperlinking, is covered in detail in Chapter 8.

A Final Note

Planning and organizing are your best friends when it comes to portfolio building. Together, if done well, they will save you hours of time and bottles of aspirin. The tools we offer in this chapter are easily adapted to any type of portfolio. We encourage you to experiment with them. The tips we provide have emerged as we have tried to help students make sense of their portfolio building efforts. As you construct your portfolio, you may find it helpful to revisit this chapter, as planning and organizing affect every part of the portfolio development process.

five
Philosophy

The Unifying Element of Portfolios

If you're not sure where you're going, you're liable to end up someplace else and not even know it.

—Robert Mager

Your Educational Philosophy

Who are you as a professional? How does your knowledge and experience shape your practice? What role has education played in your life? And why did you choose early care and education as your field and education as your profession? The answers to these questions inform your educational philosophy and, consequently, have tremendous influence on your day-to-day practice. Your philosophy is a personal clarification and articulation of your educational beliefs and values. You define yourself by it; your practice reflects it. Before we can discuss the details of your educational philosophy, though, we want to put *philosophy* in context.

Philosophy: A Quick Refresher

Philosophy is a word that is frequently used in education but infrequently explained. We believe that, in order to effectively articulate an educational philosophy, two things are important. First, you must understand what a philosophy is. Second, you must know the basis—or roots—of your values and beliefs about education. To these ends, we have defined the general construct of philosophy, located it in the context of education, and provided a brief explanation of the philosophies that are most prevalent in early care and education.

66

Philosophy as a Construct

Philosophy, in the broad sense, is a system of conscious and unconscious assumptions about the nature of humankind and the meaning of life. It is what comprises one's worldview. Worldview is highly personal. It is neither right nor wrong but is based on personal experiences and observations, and on knowledge derived from others. It asks, and answers, fundamental questions that have had deep, personal meaning to human beings since the beginning of time.

Over the centuries, likeminded people constructed distinct ways to explain the nature of life and the universe. Although they posed the same questions within metaphysical, epistemological, and axiological contexts, they arrived at different answers. As a result, a variety of philosophies emerged. Some of the oldest include idealism, realism, pragmatism, and existentialism. Figure 5.1 (adapted from Webb, Metha, & Jordan, 1992) identifies philosophical contexts through which questions are asked and answers are sought. The diagram also shows the basic questions associated with each context. These contexts include the metaphysical (pertaining to the nature of reality and the cosmos), the epistemological (addressing the nature of knowledge and knowing), and the axiological (concerned with the nature of ethics, values, and aesthetics). Although it is beyond the scope of this book to discuss Western civilization's great philosophies, suffice it to say that much of how contemporary society thinks about education is rooted in these systems of thought.

Philosophy in the Context of Education

Just as humans have constructed different, and often conflicting, philosophies to answer the grand questions about life in general, educators have built different, and often conflicting, philosophies in response to questions specific to the nature, purpose, and value of education. In this section, we focus on the educational philosophies that are most likely to be encountered in early care and education settings. In earlier chapters, we discussed two of these: Constructivism and Behaviorism. In Table 5.1 we have summarized

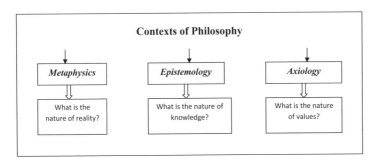

FIGURE 5.1 Contexts of Philosophy

Table 5.1 Summary of Educational Philosophies

	Metaphysics	Epistemology	Axiology	Aim of Education	Implications for Practice
Progressivism (Constructivism comes out of Progressivism.)	Reality is experience. It derives from interactions between the individual and his environment and changes over time.	Knowledge comes to be known through experimentation using the scientific method. Truth is never fully known.	What is ethically or morally good is judged on the basis of what works for the larger community. It is relative and situational.	To promote autonomy, problem solving, lifelong learning, and social responsibility.	**Teacher:** Facilitator and guide. **Student:** Self-directed, intrinsically motivated, actively engaged with the environment and with others. **Practices:** Cooperative learning, problem setting and problem solving; open-ended activities, experimentation.
Existentialism	Perception is reality. Reality is determined by each individual. People have free will.	Knowledge is personal and comes through personal choices. The individual is responsible for own knowledge.	Values are a matter of what one freely chooses and is, therefore, responsible for one's behaviors on the basis of those choices.	To recognize and accept personal responsibility. To acknowledge individuality. "March to one's own drum."	**Teacher:** Relates to each student as an individual, stresses individual responsibility and choice. **Student:** Chooses own means of expression, demonstrates personal responsibility, is at peace with own uniqueness. **Practices:** Individualizes instruction, open classroom with free choice.
Behaviorism	There is no such thing as free will. Individuals are products of their externa environment.	External stimuli are the source of all knowledge. Learning is a response to external stimuli.	Values are environmentally formed.	To promote conformity to authority, passivity.	**Teacher:** Reinforces desirable behaviors using rewards. **Student:** Follows directions, engages in programmed learning. **Practices:** Skill-and-drill exercises, mastery of discrete bits of knowledge, use of worksheets, decontextualized learning.

| Essentialism | The physical world is the basis for reality. | Knowledge is derived through application of the scientific method. | Natural and moral laws are absolute. | To produce competent and productive members of society. "Back-to basics." | **Teacher:** The center of the classroom— sets the moral standard, stays focused on the basics (eliminating anything considered nonessential), transmits knowledge. **Student:** Receives useful information as delivered by the teacher. **Practices:** Lecture on essential information, whole-group instruction on basics. |

these along with two other prominent philosophies. We have connected each philosophy to the principles within the three philosophical contexts, to their educational aims, and to their implications for educational practice.

Why go to the Trouble to Consider Philosophy?

To answer this question, look again at the definition of philosophy, this time, with education in mind:

> Philosophy is a system of conscious and unconscious assumptions about the nature of education. It is based on personal experiences and observations, and on knowledge derived from others. It asks, and answers, questions that are fundamentally important in education.

Fundamental questions for educators include: What is the aim of education? What is the nature of knowledge and knowing? Who should be educated? What is education's value to society?

Closely examining your personal experience, observations, and knowledge about education in light of these questions is a first step in uncovering the beliefs and values that motivate and direct your educational behavior. It enables you to determine "the principles that define [your] views about the learner, the teacher, and the [setting]" (Webb et al., 1992, p. 174). The answers to these questions help to establish your identity as an educator. While many educators subscribe to a particular philosophy, it is not uncommon for educators to assume a more eclectic perspective in which principles are drawn from multiple philosophies. Uncovering your beliefs and values about education brings you face to face with the principles that form your personal philosophy. Now it is time to begin building your own philosophy statement.

Philosophy Statement: The Unifying Element of Portfolios

Every portfolio must have a place from which to begin. We believe that a portfolio begins—and ultimately ends—with a carefully crafted philosophy statement. The portfolio process begins with an initial articulation of your philosophy. The statement is revised, further developed, and refined through reflection-in-action (Schon, 1983) over the course of the portfolio process. The process ends with revisiting the statement to ensure that the practice represented in the portfolio is truly reflective of, and congruent with it. Ultimately, the philosophy statement unifies all elements within the portfolio. It is the statement of who you are as a professional and what principles guide your practice.

Just What is a Philosophy Statement?

A philosophy statement is a concise, written description of your beliefs and values specific to teaching and learning. It is a personal representation—or vision—of your ideal self and the ideal practice to which you aspire. The philosophy statement serves as a blueprint—guiding you, using the personally meaningful signs and symbols you determine—toward an image of your ideal teaching/learning self. As such, the philosophy statement is not something that can be proved or disproved. It is not right or wrong. The statement is used as a reference point against which you check to see if your practice matches your beliefs, and if the evidence collected accurately and authentically reflects your practice.

What Does a Philosophy Statement do and Why is it Important?

The philosophy statement makes explicit, and publicly communicates, your philosophical point of view and theoretical groundings—the foundational ideas that are consistent with your larger worldview. It expresses the principles that guide your decision making. It also provides a foundation for congruence, a base from which to reflect on practice—past, present, and future—and against which to evaluate all actions and activities that eventually become part of the portfolio. The statement keeps the big picture in front of you, allowing you to consider how the various parts fit seamlessly into the whole. It is a tool for confirming the connection between beliefs and practice, thus preserving the integrity between beliefs and practice. It also provides a backdrop for self-evaluation and the establishment of realistic expectations and goals.

The Philosophy–Theory Connection

The great world philosophies express the general assumptions and speculations human beings have about existence. Educational philosophies constitute the beliefs and values educators have about the nature and purpose of education. Theories, on the other hand, are sets of scientifically derived principles or ideas used to explain phenomena. Theories are used to support one's philosophy. Each professional educator has an obligation to know, and to be able to articulate, his or her philosophical and theoretical roots. Clear, strong, linkages between philosophy and theory ground the philosophy statement and give an educator professional credibility. It moves the statement beyond personal opinion and connects it to something larger than oneself—the professional knowledge base.

Dispositions: Getting into the Right Frame of Mind

We have described portfolios as representing knowledge, skills, dispositions, and accomplishments. Knowledge, skills, and accomplishments can be readily observed or tested. However, *dispositions* is a concept that is harder to pin down. We want to pause a moment here to define "disposition" as, like "philosophy," it is a term often used without explanation in education.

We have all known people who had the knowledge, skills and, perhaps, talents to accomplish great things but failed to do so because they lacked the will or the discipline. They just were not inclined—or disposed—to work very hard at something in which they might otherwise have excelled.

Katz (1995) defines "dispositions" as consistent and frequent patterns of behavior wherein the individual acts intentionally, or mindfully, in particular contexts and at particular times. These "ways of responding [are] more determined by characteristics internal to the actor than provoked by the environment" (p. 51). They constitute "habits of mind," rather than "mindless habits" (p. 57). In contrast to the notion of "habits of mind," Langer (1997) defines mindlessness as "entrapment in old categories; by automatic behavior that precludes attending to new signals; and by action that operates from a single perspective. Being mindless . . . is like being on automatic pilot" (p. 4).

Considering your philosophy requires mindfulness—an intentional look at the things that move you, that shape your worldview. Therefore, it is worth a moment to assess your habits of mind in relation to teaching and learning in preparation for working on a philosophy statement.

Habits of mind—dispositions—that are useful in this process include flexibility of thought, intellectual curiosity, perseverance, risk taking, and critical reflection. We have identified these particular dispositions as important because beliefs and values are often fixed and unconscious, requiring conscious, concerted, and sustained effort to see them and state them clearly. This can be a demanding and time-consuming effort—one that is often more difficult than it appears on the surface. We find that in asking students to examine critically their "habitual ways of thinking and acting" (Brookfield, 1987, pp. 15–16), some students experience anxiety, uncertainty, defensiveness, and even anger. Emotional responses such as these are not unusual and are often part of the (holistic) Constructivist process.

We offer a few short anecdotes to illustrate the importance of reevaluating our habitual practices and making conscious decisions about what we really believe and why we believe it. The first is a story about a grown woman whose mother had come for a visit:

> The mother was sitting in the kitchen while her daughter prepared dinner. The daughter cut off both ends of the roast before putting it into the roasting

pan. Her mother watched, and then chuckled. The daughter asked what had amused her. In response, her mother asked, "Why did you cut off the ends like that?" Her daughter thought for a moment, and then replied, "When I was growing up, that's what I always saw you do." The mother chuckled again, and explained that she had cut off the ends of roasts because her roasting pan was too small for whole roasts to fit.

The moral of the story is that the daughter had continued practicing a habit that made no sense in the current context, but she had never stopped to question the practice.

A second story comes from a recent child development class. Students were studying play in the context of the preschool playground, particularly as it relates to rough-and-tumble play. The literature drew sharp distinctions between aggressive play and aggression in children. Students conducted focused observations of both in their programs over a period of weeks, then discussed their observations in light of their reading. In a reflection at the conclusion of this learning sequence, one student wrote:

> In every program I have ever worked in, the children have never been allowed to play in a rough and tumble way. At the least, it's considered rowdy behavior that is unnecessary. At the worst, it's considered aggression and kind of violent. I never questioned these ideas. I just know that everybody seems to agree that it's bad for children. After studying rough and tumble play—and really looking at the children—I realize that it has value, it's normal, and that it is really different from a play problem where a child uses aggression to get his way or take out frustration. I just never thought about it before. This experience has led to a discussion among our whole staff about play—our understanding of it and our rules about it. We are planning a staff training on it and we are talking about having it as the topic of our spring parent night.

These stories illustrate how people frequently continue doing things because, in their experience, that is how they observed them done or were told they must be done. They had never questioned why. Each of us has a professional obligation to consciously make informed decisions about best practices, and to choose from multiple approaches those that are congruent with one's own beliefs (Schon, 1983).

Philosophy Statement Essentials

Over the years we have developed guidelines to assist early care and education students and practitioners in developing philosophy statements. The guidelines for content that we delineate here meet our vision of what a

Table 5.2 Components of a Philosophy Statement

1. Philosophical Foundation: The nature, aim/s, and value of education.
2. Theoretical Foundation: The theories and/or research that ground the philosophy.
3. Learning: The sources of motivation for learning, and how people learn.
4. Roles and Relationships: The teacher's and student's roles in learning. The nature of the teacher–student relationship. The relationship between the environment and learning. The nature of your relationship with others: colleagues, parents, the community.

philosophy statement is and what it should contain. Philosophy statements should summarize the portfolio builder's philosophical and theoretical foundations, and they should address how teaching and learning practices are expressed in the context of those foundational beliefs. Table 5.2 summarizes the components of a philosophy statement. The order in which they are addressed and presented are the prerogative of each writer.

As a way to get started, we have briefly explained each component and identified some questions that you might consider in developing a philosophy statement. These are not the only questions; there may be others that occur to you as you proceed. We have also included excerpts from students' philosophy statements that illustrate the components.

Philosophical Foundation: The Nature, Aim/s, and Value of Education

Keep in mind that this component deals with the nature of reality, knowledge, and values. It is the philosophical underpinning of the statement. It answers such questions as, "What is early care and education about?", "Where does knowledge come from?", "Is it constructed or is it transmitted?", "Why does early care and education exist?", "What does it hope to achieve and for whom?", and "What value is it to society?"

Excerpts from students' statements:

Another responsibility of educators is to help students become socialized, competent, and educated.

An integral part of education is to help students become lifelong learners.

Theoretical Foundation: The Theories and/or Research that Ground the Philosophy

In model statements, clear connections are drawn between philosophical and theoretical foundations. If, for instance, you believe that children learn by doing, then the sources of theoretical support would most likely be the theories of Progressivists such as Dewey, and Constructivists such as Piaget and Vygotsky. Questions that assist in sorting out the philosophical/theoretical connections might include, "What in the early care and education knowledge base explains what you believe?" "With what research are you familiar that explains your beliefs?"

Excerpts from students' statements:

> Consistent with Piaget's theory of cognitive development, I believe that infants and toddlers learn about the world through their senses and by interacting with their environment.

> I believe that first, children's needs must be sensitively and consistently met so that they learn to trust their caregivers and develop secure attachments to them. I base this belief on both Erikson's psychosocial theory of human development and Maslow's hierarchy of needs.

Learning: The Source/s of Motivation for Learning and How People Learn

This component is at the heart of your philosophy statement. It addresses what compels people to learn and how knowledge comes to be known. It answers the questions, "*Why* do people learn? For instance, do you believe that children are basically motivated to learn due to intrinsic desires and natural curiosity? Or, instead, do you believe that learning is motivated by external forces? What do you believe about *how* people, in general, learn? Do you believe that learning is an active or a passive process on the part of the learner? Does knowledge come from one's interactions with the world, or as a result of one person transmitting knowledge to another?"

Excerpts from students' statements:

> Children are born with a natural curiosity to experiment with, explore, and investigate their environment.

> Because most children are intrinsically motivated, they will want to learn as much about themselves and their environment as they can.

Roles and Relationships: The Teacher's and Student's Roles in Learning; The Nature of the Teacher–Student Relationship; The Relationship Between the Environment and Learning; The Nature of Your Relationships with Others: Colleagues, Parents, the Community

How you see the teacher's role should be congruent with your beliefs about the source of motivation for learning and about how you believe learning occurs. If, for instance, you believe that students are active learners, and that learning is driven by natural curiosity, then the teacher's role could be to facilitate, coach, foster, and encourage. If you believe that students are passive learners who learn best when the learning is transmitted and reinforced by others, then the teacher's role could be to lecture, reward, praise, dictate. What do you believe the teacher's role is in relationship to students' learning?

Excerpts from students' statements:

> The teacher should initiate learning by creating interest, sparking curiosity, and guiding the learning process.

> The role of the teacher is to respect the children, to meet their needs and to establish a safe, stimulating environment which invites children to explore. Many different experiences should be provided to promote growth in every area of children's development, while the teacher stays close by to encourage the children's explorations, help them recognize boundaries and celebrate the joy of their discoveries.

Just as your view of the teacher's role should be congruent with your beliefs about the source of motivation for learning and what you believe about how learning occurs, so must the student's role be congruent. Burk and Dunn (1996) suggest that "Constructivists view autonomy as the aim of education" (p. 11). If you subscribe to this view, then the student's role coulds include active engagement on his own behalf, questioning authority and setting and solving problems.

Excerpts from students' statements:

> In the classroom, it is the responsibility of the students to participate in creating the classroom rules and therefore maintain their behavior.

> The role of the children is to explore and interact with their surroundings, to make choices based on their interests, and to master their bodies while learning to stay within boundaries.

Different philosophies ascribe different roles to the environment and its place in learning. What part do you believe the environment plays in learning? Is it the source of learning, as the Behaviorists believe? Does it support and facilitate learning, as the Constructivists believe?

Excerpts from students' statements:

> I believe that the environment should be safe, stimulating, and should invite children to explore.

> The environment plays an important part in children's learning. It supports their curiosity and it reflects their interests.

How do you see yourself in relation to others in the learning environment? Are you a partner with parents in children's learning? Do you see the community as an integral part of the learning environment, or as something separate from and beyond the scope of the classroom? Do you view colleagues as supports, collaborators, resources? Do you value teamwork, or do you prefer more solitary enterprise? Considering how you conceive of the learning environment and its role in children's learning is essential.

Excerpts from students' statements:

> I believe that the neighborhood is an extension of the classroom and offers many opportunities to enrich the curriculum.

> Collaboration and teamwork between parents and the school are essential to effective education for children. I am committed to meaningful parent and community involvement in my classroom.

Sample Philosophy Statements

Many of the examples just given illustrate discrete parts of components of a philosophy statement in order to make the meaning of each clear. Several excerpts address more than one aspect of a component or more than one component. Keep in mind that your goal is ultimately to integrate all of the components, in total, into a seamless statement. We have included two sample statements that illustrate this integration. Although their authors teach at different levels, each statement incorporates the four elements: philosophical foundation, theoretical foundation, learning motivation and process, and the roles and relationships in learning.

Laurel's Philosophy Statement (Preservice, Elementary School)

> I believe that all children have a natural curiosity and the ability to learn. As a teacher it is my job to foster this curiosity through education of the whole child, in mind, body and spirit. Therefore, the environment we provide should be one that encourages this natural curiosity. If done so, children will exercise their abilities with great personal success.

> As a teacher, it is my job to make sure the environment is appropriate for all learners and to help children make meaningful connections. It is my job to find a way to bring out the individual talents that exists inside each child so that each one becomes a lifelong learner, fulfills his or her potential, and becomes a contributing member of our society.

> Children learn when curriculum is meaningful. Children learn by doing. They achieve understanding by exploring and experimenting with their own ideas. This

can be achieved by a classroom environment that uses many hands-on and project based activities.

I believe that instruction must be differentiated so that each child can use his or her own special "intelligence" and achieve success. I will be sensitive to the many different skills, preferences, and inclinations of different children, what one well-known researcher, Gardner, calls "intelligences," because I know that children learn in many different ways.

Based on the work of a second researcher, Maslow, I feel it is my job to make sure children are safe in my classroom, both physically and emotionally. In this way children will be open to taking risks. It is the job of the student to be an active learner, a risk taker, and a sharing, cooperating member of the classroom community.

My classroom will be child-centered with children's artwork displayed on the walls. Children will work in cooperative groups. Students will be engaged as a result of using developmentally appropriate curriculum. It is my goal to have students truly value learning. If I can do that, I will have given them the tools for success and I will have pointed them in the right direction.

Krishna's Philosophy Statement (Preschool)

My experience in working with children and families, along with my education on how children develop, has enabled me to construct a strong philosophy. It is based on my beliefs of how children learn best. Vygotsky has stated that with the guidance of a sensitive caregiver, who guides the transition from assisted performance to independent achievement, a child gains the sense that "I can." My goal is to facilitate each individual child's learning by challenging him or her at the appropriate level. My belief system is congruent with the point of view that a responsibility of educators is to help students become socialized, competent, and educated.

Children come into the world like a sponge, taking in everything. As they grow, their inborn desire to learn is heightened. So, by providing each child with meaningful, appropriate opportunities to build on their previous experiences and schemas, learning takes place. I believe that through using their senses and with hands-on, active play in a fun, open atmosphere, children are able to gain a better understanding of themselves and their work. Through play they are able to master skills, which helps build their positive self-concept.

My role as an educator of young children is to provide a supportive and safe environment from which to explore, to enable each child the opportunity to reach their full potential. I feel that by establishing a strong relationship with the children and their families, I am better equipped to give each child what he or she needs and wants, and also demonstrate my respect for the wishes of the family. By modeling respect, patience, and love for each individual person (child or adult), I am providing a base from which my relationships stem and my lessons begin. The children are then able to actively engage in their environment through materials and interactions with others and to make choices that develop who they are. I believe that the environment should be stimulating, culturally sensitive, full of positive messages, and provide open-ended experiences and opportunities to problem-solve and wonder.

All my life I've felt a deep desire to help others. As an adult I've decided to dedicate my life to creating our future generation. My goal is to guide each child so that, with a deep sense of "I can," he or she will go out and do. I truly believe in the power of positive guidance and acceptance for all the world's creatures. I plan to provide a healthy and positive first experience in the lives of children from all walks of life. This is my passion, my calling, to the world of children.

A Final Note

Philosophy statements are born from close self-examination of those things that silently direct and guide an educator's actions. Clarifying your philosophy frees you to make informed, consistent choices in your practice. By communicating your philosophy, you tell others what they can expect from you, and it serves as a reminder to you of your vision of ideal practice and ideal self.

six
Reflection

The Defining Feature of Portfolios

Learning without thought is labor lost; thought without learning is perilous.

—Confucius

We characterize reflection as the defining feature of portfolios because it is the mental process through which human beings convert experience into personal knowledge. It is reflection that distinguishes portfolios from scrapbooks or other kinds of collections. Reflections form a continuous thread that runs through the portfolio, tying artifacts to learning, and providing evidence of growth and change over time.

Reflection serves several important purposes. It helps you to do the following.

1. Bring experience and knowledge together to produce new learning that is personally meaningful.
2. Connect theory to practice.
3. Strengthen a critical reflection disposition.
4. Gain insight into your learning and personal/professional development.
5. Manage your emotions throughout the learning process.

Reflection is a bridge between the cognitive and emotional states. It is a useful mechanism for examining the emotional impact of cognitively oriented content. As Mezirow (1991) explains, "Reflection is the central dynamic involved in problem solving, problem posing, and transformation of meaning schemes and meaning perspectives" (p. 116).

Prerequisites for Reflection

Reflection, like *philosophy*, is a word that is used more and more in education and other professional settings, but is too often left undefined and decontextualized. Students and practitioners alike are asked to do more of it, but often have only a vague notion of what it is. We identify reflection as central to, and inextricable from, the portfolio process. As such, we think it is important for readers to understand how we interpret and contextualize reflection. To that end, we have addressed reflection from several vantage points: as a disposition, as a human capability, and as a cognitive skill that has application in, and is necessary to, professional practice.

In the previous chapter, we identified a number of dispositions (ways in which a person is inclined to behave) that we consider key to the portfolio process. Being critically reflective is one of these dispositions. In addition to being a disposition, we also see reflection as a human capability—that is, as a universal human potential. The capacity to reflect is a characteristic unique to human beings. It is one of the things that distinguishes humans from all other creatures. Even so, some people do not develop the capacity; it is not automatic. Many who do develop it use it circumstantially and to greater or lesser degrees in different areas of their lives.

Developing the capability for critical reflection requires higher order thinking skills, conscious engagement, and sustained effort. Four aspects of thinking (higher order skills) make reflection possible. The first of these is *abstract thinking*: a mental process whereby concepts that cannot be experienced directly through the senses can be understood, such as friendship and trust. The second is *complex thinking*: the ability to perceive multiple aspects or multiple levels of a problem or situation at the same time. The third is *metacognition*: awareness, not just of a problem or situation, but of one's thinking about one's thoughts on a problem or situation. It is thinking about thinking. The fourth is *pragmatism*: the ability to adapt logical thinking to the practical constraints of real-life situations and manage the ambiguity that often accompanies them (Arnett, 2004). These cognitive abilities usually begin to emerge in early adolescence. They develop over time and are enhanced through use, combined with modeling, mentoring, and instruction.

Reflection in Practice

We have briefly described reflection as a capability that humans possess, a disposition that some acquire, and a cognitive skill enabled by higher order thinking. Now we are going to talk about it as an essential professional practice.

Anthony Clark (as reported in Lyons, 1998) describes reflection as "thematic constructions of meaning taking place over time and drawn from multiple experiences" (p. 106). Clark's use of the phrase "thematic constructions of meaning" is instructive, in that it provokes an image of contemplating related behaviors to form a picture of how one habitually behaves in certain circumstances. For instance, how might a teacher think about and understand her interactions with parents generally? What does her examination of her behaviors with, or attitudes about, parents reveal to her about herself? How does she interpret her experiences with parents? What new information does she have that might influence her usual behaviors or ways of dealing with parents?

Clark goes on to say that, "reflection ought to be considered as a drawing together of long strands of connections, the weaving together of experiences, theory, and practices into meaning for the individual . . . a kind of construction of knowledge" (Lyons, 1998, p. 106). Here, he captures an important essence of reflection: The making of contextual meaning out of one's experience. Experience in this sense is the combination of one's prior knowledge, day-to-day experiences (past and present), and new knowledge. Learning, in large part, can be thought of as experience that has been reflected on. As Posner (2005) notes, "We do not actually learn from experience as much as we learn from reflecting on experience" (p. 21). We agree with both Clark and Posner. We define critical reflection as:

> the practice of intentionally bringing into conscious awareness one's motivations, thoughts, beliefs, questions, assumptions, feelings, attitudes, desires, and expectations for the purpose of gaining insightful understanding as to their meaning, their connections to what is personally known, and in light of new experiences and information. Reflection makes possible the insights necessary to learn from experience and alter habitual behaviors.

As the definition indicates, intentionality, or purposefulness, is an aspect of reflection. Without purpose, reflection is hollow—perhaps just random mental wanderings. We reflect on our actions and the actions of others with the intention of uncovering our motives, assumptions, beliefs, and the like, so that we may gain deeper understanding and make sense of things—to fit them into, or build new, constructs.

Behavior stems from one's motivations, thoughts, beliefs, questions, assumptions, feelings, attitudes, desires, and expectations. Reflection is a tool for the analysis of our observations and actions, their consequences, and their implications. Reflection aids us in imagining alternative ways of acting. It is a mechanism by which we can challenge ourselves to ask critical, and sometimes, life-changing questions. Reflection also allows us to go beyond ourselves—to challenge prevailing social, political, cultural, and professional beliefs and practices (Brookfield, 1995). Reflection is a tool for personal change. It is also a tool for social change.

Reflection and Learning Frames

For purposes of portfolios, reflection is particularly well applied to three key learning frames. The approach you take to your written reflections may vary according to the learning frame that best applies. The learning frames include these:

1. Experiences you have as an observer of self and others.
2. Experiences you have as a critical reader of the professional literature.
3. Experiences you have as an implementer of activities.

Experiences You have as an Observer of Self and Others

This frame is relationship oriented. The experiences you have as an observer of self and others encompass intrapersonal and interpersonal interactions. Intrapersonal interactions include observations you make of, and conversations you have with, yourself on matters of importance to you. Interpersonal interactions are those that include observations you make of, and with, others, such as those between yourself and a parent, between yourself and a child or group of children, between two children, between a child and teacher, or within a group of children. This frame concentrates on the qualities and content of relationships within the context of events.

Experiences You have as a Critical Reader of the Professional Literature

Part of becoming a professional is learning to engage the literature rather than simply being a consumer of it. This learning frame focuses on both the rigor with which you explore the professional literature, and the disposition you bring to your reading of it. So often students have been taught to read for key points, memorize the key points, and produce them in some fashion on an exam. This approach strips reading of its meaning and value. Engaging the literature—reading critically—requires adopting an inquiring frame of mind. The critical reader asks questions such as, "What is the author really saying, and from what perspective?", "What does this mean to me?", "How is this important?", "How does this relate to my experience and/or prior knowledge?", "How does this fit with what I believe?", "How can I use this information?", "What questions does this raise for me?", and "What else do I want to know about this?"

Experiences You have as an Implementer of Activities

In producing artifacts for your portfolio, you will most likely conduct activities in conjunction with others—children and adults. This experience frame encompasses the experiences you have while conducting those activities. It focuses on the processes and products associated with your activities. For instance, this frame addresses issues related to the success, failure, challenges, strong and weak points, outcomes, and benefits of the activities as they apply to the criteria you are attempting to satisfy.

Experience frames are not mutually exclusive. A given experience may have aspects of two, or all three. In writing a reflection, consider the criterion you are addressing and what you are trying to convey. This will suggest the frame to which you may want to direct your primary attention.

Understanding what reflection can mean for you as a professional is the first step in making it a regular feature of your practice. Yet, knowing its importance and value can still leave you wondering how to go about it. In the next section, we discuss the components of reflection and offer several tools to assist you in structuring your written reflections.

Becoming Accomplished in Written Reflection

As with any skill, written reflection lies on a continuum, from developing to accomplished (Figure 6.1). And, as with any skill, becoming accomplished at it requires practice. Fink (2003) states that reflective writing, "when viewed as a process and when done properly, has a unique ability to develop the

FIGURE 6.1 Reflection Continuum

interior life of the writer. . . . [It] focuses on the writer's learning experience itself and attempts to identify the significance and meaning of a given learning experience, primarily for the writer" (pp. 116–117). The act of reflective writing, in a sense, forces the writer to examine, clarify, and crystallize thoughts and ideas that might otherwise be floating around the mind in disconnected fragments.

The process involved in reflection has four steps (Figure 6.2). Each step plays an important role in your learning and self-actualization. As you prepare to write each reflection, consider the experience on which you are reflecting in the context of the most salient learning frame, and focus on it through each step in the reflection process. The steps in the reflection process include the following.

1. Observation and description.
2. Analysis and interpretation.
3. Insights and implications.
4. Projections and planning.

Observation and Description

Observation is at the heart of reflection. Your observations, of yourself and others in the context of your practice, form the basis of the descriptions on which you base your written reflections. When reflecting on your state of knowledge, skill, or disposition in relation to new knowledge or experience,

FIGURE 6.2 Four-Step Process of Reflection

you will want to describe where you were—in knowing and feeling—prior to that new exposure.

Even without being aware of it, you are constantly observing what goes on around you and trying to make sense of it. Human beings seek and order patterns in their physical and emotional environments, and try to fit them into existing patterns. Some of the observations you make will stand out for you. They will intrigue you, bother you, delight you, or concern you. They will fit your existing patterns, or they will violate them. The experiences that stand out for you are the ones to write about, because these are the ones that probably have meaning for you on some level. If you are unable to jot down notes on the spot (a running record), make notes as soon after the event as possible (an anecdotal record). Our minds lose track of details very quickly. Flesh out the details at your earliest opportunity in order to capture the most complete and accurate account. This stage of the process can take as little as a few minutes each day.

Descriptions of an observable event embody the same qualities as any good observation done for educational purposes. They are factual, objective, and concise. Curtis and Carter (2000) identify five qualities of a good observation, shown below.

1. Objectivity (seeing without judging, as though you were a camera lens).
2. Directness (recording direct quotes whenever possible).
3. Specificity (specific details: who was involved, when and where the action took place, your involvement in the event, and what actually happened).
4. Completeness (the story with a beginning, a middle, and an end, however brief).
5. Mood (the social and emotional details without interpretation: tone of voice, body language, facial expressions, hand gestures).

Descriptions do not include the assignation of motive, emotion, intentions, capabilities, or traits, even if they are your own. This first step in the process asks that you temporarily set aside your analysis (what you think was going on), interpretation (why you think it was going on), and judgment (whether you think it was right or wrong).

Those who are new to reflective writing often mistake description for reflection. This is why initial attempts at reflection often resemble summaries of facts or book reports, sometimes with unintentional interpretation and judgment mixed in. Keep in mind that the function of description in reflective writing is to establish the context of the event and to provide adequate detail that sets the stage for the analysis, interpretation, projection, and planning that follow.

Analysis and Interpretation

Analysis and interpretation involve careful examination of the motivations, thoughts, beliefs, questions, assumptions, feelings, attitudes, desires, and expectations that guide your thinking and behavior. Through analysis and interpretation, you consciously examine the "whys" behind your actions and the genesis of your thoughts and beliefs. The incidents or experiences you describe in a reflection may be representative of your habitual ways of thinking and acting in similar circumstances. Explore possible connections between your current and past actions and ideas. Carefully consider how what you have observed connects to, and is directed by, your motives, and so on. This is where insight comes from. Be thoughtful about how your experiences align with the theories you hold or with theories with which you have become newly acquainted. Bridging theory and practice is a challenge that this process can facilitate. Examine the impact of your observations on your personal beliefs and behaviors. This step can open the door to personal and professional transformation.

Making sense of an experience and coming to understand its impact do not always happen quickly. The sifting and sorting process can take a little time. Having some distance from an event provides the mental breathing space the mind needs to process the experience. We encourage students to set aside time at the end of each week to review their descriptions, check in on their mental wanderings, and write their reflections.

Insights and Implications

What have you learned from a given experience about yourself, about your practice, and about others? What has become clearer to you? The insight born of reflection offers a window into everyday experiences that are easily taken for granted. The familiar is often the overlooked. Yet, your careful, thoughtful appraisal of it can shed light on the truths that lie within.

No one operates in a vacuum. Your actions affect not only you, but also others around you. They can have a ripple effect—sometimes having an impact on people whom you have not met. Think about the outcomes and implications of your actions and observations. Consider the results of what you do on yourself and on those immediately affected by your actions. Anticipate the effects on those who may experience the consequences of your actions at a later time (e.g., the children who will be in your program next year who will benefit from a policy decision you make today). Insight fuels change.

Projection and Planning

How can the conclusions you draw be used to improve your practice now and in the future? Examine the insights you have gained in light of your philosophy statement and your current practices. Consider what your reflection has taught you and frame it against the vision you have of your ideal self and your ideal practice. What will you change? What has been validated? Contemplate the meaning of specific learning experiences in relation to the criteria to which you are being held. Use your insights to consider how what you have learned has changed you and what that may mean to your future. Determine the relevance and implications of your learning with regard to future action. In projection and planning, you answer the questions "So what (that I've learned this)?", and "Now what (do I do with it)?" This step moves you to action.

If you are new to writing reflectively, or to the steps we have discussed above, you might wonder how it all looks in a real reflection. In the next section, we have dissected a reflection to show you how one student incorporated and integrated the four steps.

Anatomy of a Reflection

You might look at the steps in the reflection process discussed above and wonder how you can cover all of those steps and still have time in your day for anything else! Reflective writing does take time and effort. However, written reflections do not have to be exhaustive tomes. They can be relatively brief pieces and still be effective. Manny's reflection (Figure 6.3) is one such

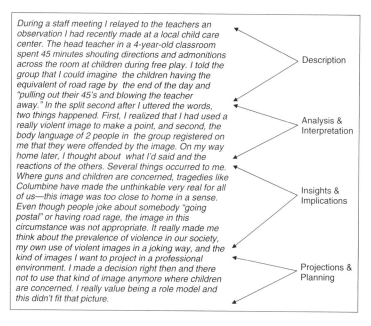

FIGURE 6.3 Manny's Reflection

example. We have pointed out where and how the steps of reflection were used (description; analysis and interpretation; insights and implications; and projections and planning).

Tools for Written Reflection

We have devised several tools to help students structure their reflections. The first tool has two parts: an Observation Form (Figure 6.4), and an Observation Follow-Up (Figure 6.5). The Observation Form includes columns for the

OBSERVATION FORM
Observation #: _____
Your Name Setting Observation Method Date/Time (start to finish) Child being observed Others Involved Nature of Episode Focus of observation
Be mindful of your choice of words (see explanatory notes and sample words at the bottom of each column).

DESCRIPTION	MEMOS
	Interpretive words: *Words that indicate thoughts, beliefs, motivations, questions, assumptions, emotions, attitudes, desires, and/or expectations* (e.g., seems, thinks, wants, appears, likes, believes, meant to, feels, it looks like, sad, on purpose, intentionally)
Descriptive words: *Words that convey action and the quality of an action. Use active verbs, adjectives, and adverbs* (e.g., hurried, squatted, gingerly, screeched, tossed, grabbed, pushed, firmly, roughly, busily, struggled)	**Judgmental words:** *Words that places a value on an action or person or assigns a trait or capability* (e.g., wrong, right, good, bad, nice, mean, honest, smart, pretty, trustworthy, spoiled)

Analysis
Connect what you observed to relevant theories and empirical findings. Be specific. Use citations. Validate connections with examples from your observations.
Reflection Discuss insights you've had, and their source, about yourself or the child you observed.
References (APA style)

FIGURE 6.4 Observation Log

description of the event, interpretation, and judgment—a physical reminder to discriminate among these three mental functions. Each section contains prompts and hints to assist the observer with the observation task. The log can be used for on-the-spot observations (running records) or for recording events after the fact (anecdotal records).

The Observation Follow-Up assists students with the sorting out of the analysis and interpretation, insights and implications, and projections and planning aspects of the reflection. It also includes prompts to help students focus on what is most pertinent in each area.

We encourage students to use the Observation Form and Observation Follow-Up on at least a weekly basis, or more often as events of note arise. When used consistently over a period of time, these two documents, used

Your name:		
Date:		
OBSERVATION FOLLOW-UP		
(Form # _____)		
Analysis & Interpretation How has what I observed & described, and my analysis and interpretation of it affected me? How have I been changed by it? What remains the same? What biases have I noticed? What is the source of my feelings about this event?	**Insights & Implications** What have I learned about myself? What has this made me question? What has it validated? How am I the same or different? What do my analysis & interpretation imply for my future behavior and thinking?	**Projections & Planning** What will I do differently? What will remain the same? Where am I going in my practice as a result of what I've learned?

FIGURE 6.5 Observation Follow-Up

in tandem, constitute a field journal. The field journal can then serve as an excellent tool for longer-term or more global reflection.

In addition to the Observation Form and Observation Follow-Up, we provide students with a rubric for assessing their reflections (Table 6.1). The rubric is the scoring guide, or criteria, against which the reflections are assessed.

Another tool we have found helpful to students in writing their reflections is "Where I started—Where I am—What's next?" This set of prompts is often used when helping students engage the professional literature, and make sense of it in their individual contexts—the second learning frame. It is also effective when used to reflect on the implementation of an activity—the third learning frame. The example below illustrates the third learning frame. An intern in a teacher education program wrote it. She was reflecting on her efforts at "understanding and organizing subject matter for student learning," a content area in the state credentialing standards.

Zhling's Reflection

Where I Started . . .
As a novice teacher the biggest challenge for me was to make curriculum comprehensible to my special education students. Although I was comfortable with

Table 6.1 Reflection Rubric

	Developing	Competent	Exemplary
Observation and Description	May not include all parts. Language is not descriptive. Confuses interpretation and judgment with description.	Includes all parts, but with only some rich description. Mixes in some interpretation or judgment.	Employs all parts (complete, objective, direct, specific, mood) to tell the story. Uses rich, descriptive language. No interpretation or judgment.
Analysis and Interpretation	Little evidence of exploration and clarification of thoughts, beliefs, motives, assumptions, feelings, attitudes, desires, and/or expectations. Little evidence of examination of their meaning.	Shows some evidence of exploration and clarification of thoughts, beliefs, motives, assumptions, feelings, attitudes, desires, and/or expectations. Some examination of their meaning.	Explores and clarifies thoughts, beliefs, motives, assumptions, feelings, attitudes, desires, and/or expectations related to the event. Examines what these mean on personal and professional levels.
Insights and Implications	Little insight into self. Little if any reference to change that has taken place, what remains the same, how experiences have affected him/her. Little indication of awareness of implications as to how experiences will affect future.	Some insight into self. Indicates change that has taken place, what remains the same, how experiences have affected him/her. Indicates implications with some reference to how experiences will affect future.	Demonstrates excellent insight into self. Indicates change that has taken place, what remains the same, how experiences have affected him/her. Explains implications of experience for future.
Projections and Planning	Little if any evidence of projection based on experience. Scant evidence of planning for future actions in relation to the learning gained from the experience.	Some projection based on experience. Some evidence of planning for future actions in relation to the learning gained from the experience.	Clear projections into future in reference to the experience. Evidence of plan in relation to future practice.

the subject matter, making it connect to the student was difficult. I learned that social needs are just as important and needing to be taught as are academics. I learned by trial and error in organizing curriculum and using teaching strategies. I was limited to resources that I could pull from. I didn't have a lot of supplementary materials at hand.

Where I Am . . .

I am now in a position where I can make connections from my past experiences as a teacher to help me in present situations. I've formed good relationships with my students and have learned to allow their needs to drive my instruction. I allow my students to develop as critical thinkers by presenting them with reasoning practice. I've learned that when enthusiasm is there on the part of the teacher, the students are more able to receive the lesson. My planning includes interrelating subjects to make learning meaningful and supportive.

What's Next?

In this domain, I need to build up my resources and materials in order to provide my students with different avenues to learn. I understand that with time, I will be able to collect a library of resources to use with my students.

Those who are new to reflective writing often have trouble getting started. In order to help students jump-start their writing, we devised a set of writing prompts (Table 6.2). These can be used as practice exercises or as a "crib sheet" when working with Observation Follow-Ups or other tools.

Table 6.2 Prompts to Jump-Start Reflective Writing

_____ motivated me to. . .

I thought. . ., but. . .

I believed that. . .

_____ has made me question. . .

The question this raises for me is. . .

I always assumed that. . .

On the basis of. . ., I assumed. . .

_____ makes me feel like. . .

I feel/felt that. . .

I realized that. . .

_____ makes/made me realize that. . .

My expectation was that. . .

I wanted. . .

When it happened/didn't happen, I. . .

My views on. . . have been. . .

I imagined. . .

It surprised me to find out that . . .

_____ caused me wonder about. . .and that led me to. . .

_____ is important to me because. . .

_____ has affected the way I think/feel about. . .

A Final Note

Philosophy, the blueprint of the portfolio, and reflection, its defining feature, work hand in hand to clarify and express that which lies beneath the surface of your practice. The unseen forces—values and beliefs—that are exposed and examined through reflection find expression in your philosophy statement. Once known and shared, they can become powerful tools in strengthening your practice and making it more informed and intentional.

seven
Building a Portfolio

What we have to do is to be forever curiously testing new opinions and courting new impressions.

—Walter Pater

In this chapter, we explore and illustrate how criteria frame the portfolio structure and direct its content. We explain how criteria and portfolios are connected and show you the steps that will help you get from thinking and action to a finished document that represents both. As in previous chapters, we take the time to explain the meaning of well-worn, but often not well-defined terms in an effort to arrive at a common understanding for purposes of this text. Evidence is one such word.

What is Evidence?

We use *evidence* as a broad-spectrum word to describe all of the components of the portfolio that support the builder's claims of competence with regard to knowledge, skills, dispositions, and accomplishments. We include in it every item that contributes to a reader's understanding of what you can do in your professional capacity. We divide evidence into two general categories: personal documents and artifacts.

- Personal documents are descriptive of who you are.
- Artifacts are descriptive of what you know, what you can do, and what you have done.

Table 7.1 lists examples of evidence including personal documents and artifacts. This is not meant to be a comprehensive list, nor are the items listed in order of importance or value.

Table 7.1 Examples of Evidence

Personal Documents	Artifacts
Résumés	Work samples
Philosophy statements	Observations
Reflections	Lesson plans and units
Professional development certificates	Photographs
Awards	Assessment plans
Evaluations	Field work logs or journals
Letters of reference	Audio or video clips
Certificates of membership in professional associations	Newsletters
Transcripts	Case studies
Professional growth plans	Parent handbook

Evidence is all about communication. You use it to represent and communicate connections between your beliefs and actions, thinking and doing, and artifacts and criteria. Evidence is the tangible proof that your beliefs and principles are being consistently practiced. It includes reflection on your learning and growth in relation to your practice. And it documents the connections you have made between the artifacts you collect and the criteria that you are trying to meet. Figures 7.1, 7.2, 7.3, 7.4, 7.5, and 7.6 show a variety of evidence that Juli used in her portfolio to document her development of infant and toddler curriculum and the education and involvement strategies she employed with the children's parents. Figures 7.1 and 7.2 are examples

Reflection on Professional Growth

Upon entering this cohort, my mind set was to complete the required classes and get my degree. I was not at all expecting to leave this cohort with not only such a dramatic change within my professional life, but also my home life. Every class that I have taken in this option has effected the center that I work in. From developing trainings to conducting a case study, I have been given the opportunity to affect the center in a positive way. This nontraditional class has had a far more greater impact on me than any class that I have taken before. I have formed friendships with people who have given me insight to different ways of interpreting information when dealing with children, their families, and their community. Most importantly they have now become a wonderful resource for me.

I use to be a a childcare provider who thought her way was the only way, this narrow mindedness coming solely from my own life experiences. I am now a childcare provider who opens herself to the many possibilities and even if I may not agree with certain differences I still respect them.

Hernandez Family

FIGURE 7.1 Juli's Reflection on Personal Growth

Reflection on my journey to find an appropriate curriculum for infants & toddlers

Before taking part in this program, I had never fully comprehended the concept of what a curriculum for an infant and toddler program should look like. With all the child development classes I had taken, only one or two focused on infant and toddler care. Curriculum wasn't even mentioned. When using curriculum with infants and toddlers, it was always similar to preschool curriculum. Now I know that infant/toddler curriculum is different than in a preschool setting.

Curriculum for infants and toddlers revolves around attachment and routines.

When putting this type of curriculum into practice, the child's individual needs for nurturing, security,& learning will be met.

FIGURE 7.2 Juli's Reflection on Infant and Toddler Curriculum

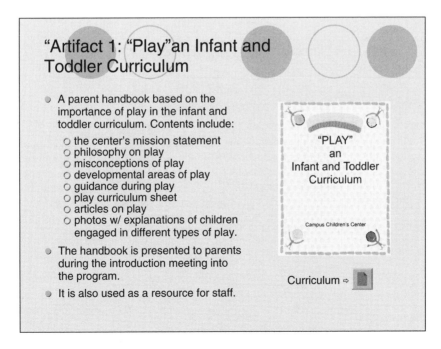

FIGURE 7.3 Juli's Parent Handbook on Curriculum

Artifact 2: Documented Play Collages

- This is a sample of one of the many collages that I posted in my classroom. Each collage shows the children engaged in play, along with a description of the importance to children's learning.

- The purpose of the collages was to grab the attention of the parents and educate them about the connection between play and learning.

FIGURE 7.4 Juli's Play Collages

Artifact 3: What I did Today!

- "What I did Today" is posted outside the classroom each day to inform parents about what occurred in their child's day.
  It tells parents
  - With my senses I...
  - With my friends I...
  - Outdoors I...
  - I used my words when I...
- Parents come to understand that infant/toddler learning is not about flashcards or the ABC song.
  Infant/toddler learning is an everyday experience created by an enriching environment and nurturing relationships with the caregivers.

FIGURE 7.5 Juli's "What I did Today!" Board

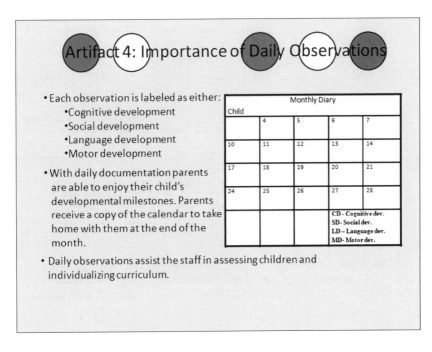

FIGURE 7.6 Juli's Daily Observation Log

of personal documents—Juli's reflections on her overall professional growth and on her more specific learning and development related to her work with infant and toddler curriculum. Figures 7.3–7.6 show examples of artifacts Juli included that validate her competency in several standards. The standards she met through the work represented in these artifacts and personal documents are shown in Figure 7.7. The next section of this chapter offers guidelines that will assist you in developing, collecting, and using evidence effectively.

General Guidelines for Selecting and Using Evidence

We have identified five general guidelines for selecting and using evidence that apply to every type of portfolio.

1. All evidence should express the voice of the builder.
2. All evidence should connect back to, and support, the purpose of the portfolio.
3. Each piece of evidence should be weighed against criteria to determine best fit.
4. Evidence must be explained clearly to communicate connections and relevance to criteria and/or philosophy.
5. The body of chosen evidence should be evaluated to ensure balanced coverage of all criteria.

Standards Met

- **Standard 1. Promoting Child Development and Learning**
- Action research, reading, and a conference on the relationship between infant toddler development & curriculum

- **Standard 2. Building Family and Community Relationships**
- Developing new ways to communicate with parents about what goes on with their children during the day

- **Standard 3: Observing, Documenting & Assessing**
- Daily observations on children & personalized monthly calendars charting development

- **Standard 4. Teaching and Learning**
- Designing curriculum around routines, relationships, & children's individual needs

FIGURE 7.7 Standards Met in Juli's Infant-Toddler Curriculum Project

All Evidence Should Express the Voice of the Builder

The evidence is an honest and accurate representation of *your* work, learning, and accomplishments at a given point in time. Even though there may be others who interact with you in your learning process and learning environments—co-teachers, instructors, master teachers, supervisors, and the like—the evidence is about you and your understandings and practices. The bottom line is that the portfolio—through the evidence—must reflect you and be congruent with your philosophy. At times we all find ourselves faced with the dilemma of being asked or expected to behave in ways that are inconsistent with our philosophies. This is not an uncommon occurrence. Although this can prove challenging, particularly in situations where you do not have ultimate control, you must remain true to yourself. The brief example below illustrates such a situation relayed by Kendra, who was engaged in building a portfolio for a college course. She had recently been hired at a child care center to co-teach a group of 3-year-olds with a teacher who had been practicing for years.

> Helen, my co-teacher, got an art experience ready for the children. The night before, she had made a sample of a collage for the children to follow. It had a brown tree trunk, a green top, and five red circles she said were apples.

She insisted that the children place the precut apples on the top of precut trees just like the sample. Each child could only have five circles and one tree. The children were supposed to put the apples on small dabs of glue that the teacher put on the paper. The children couldn't even decide where the glue went. Even though I helped the children with the project, it bothered me that it was so structured and controlled. It didn't even seem like any fun for anyone.

Helen's "one right way" approach conflicted with Kendra's philosophy of a more creative, child-directed approach. Successfully addressing this situation with Helen, and later addressing it in her portfolio, required tact, professionalism, and reflection-in-action. Kendra followed through with the art project as prescribed by her co-teacher. In her portfolio, Kendra included two art samples: the one Helen had planned and a subsequent project she had planned. Without casting aspersions on Helen or her philosophy, Kendra compared the two projects in relation to her own philosophy, pointing out why hers was more congruent than the other with her beliefs about the way children learn. The reflection that accompanied the art samples in her portfolio demonstrated Kendra's mindfulness in a difficult situation, her insights, and her flexibility.

Later in the day, I asked Helen if she always does art this way. She said she does. She said it helps children learn to follow directions and learn about how things really look. She said this was a very important part of preschool. She seemed so sure about what she believes. I realized that I don't believe the same things she does about the purpose of art. I didn't want to tell her that her way is wrong, and I didn't want her to tell me that either. What she said made me think about what I do believe about art and what I think preschool is about.

After a while, we talked again. I explained that I like more open-ended art experiences because they allow children to be creative, make decisions about how they want their pictures to look, and explore the materials. I asked her if we could switch off doing art—she could plan it one week and I would plan it the next week. That way, the children could have different kinds of experiences that would teach them different things. She agreed, and I was so relieved. Now I feel like we can each do what we think is right and the children will benefit.

Through that experience, Kendra examined her beliefs and questioned her practice in light of the practice of her co-teacher. Her reflection-in-action enabled her to introduce a compromise while still respectfully accepting Helen's point of view. She used the art samples to draw comparisons between different educational philosophies, making clear why she favored hers. So, while her artifacts included an art project that did not fit her philosophy, she used supporting evidence—her explanation and reflection—to clarify the inconsistency and to show her thinking, reasoning, decision making, connection making, and planning. It showed who *she* is in the context of her immediate circumstances.

All Evidence Should Connect Back to, and Support, the Purpose of the Portfolio

Keep the purpose of the portfolio in mind as you select representative evidence. Just as you will gauge evidence against your philosophy statement to determine coherence and consistency between them, you must also evaluate

Table 7.2 Portfolio Types and Purposes, and the Nature of their Respective Evidence

Type	Purpose of Portfolio	Nature of the Evidence	Samples of Evidence
Developmental	Facilitate and chart development	Selected sample showing incremental learning and growth over time in specific areas	Multiple drafts of philosophy statement, serial observations, reflective writings
Showcase	Highlight performance and capabilities	Projects that illustrate integration of knowledge, skills, and dispositions articulated across criteria	Parent handbook; staff training plan on play in the preschool curriculum
Assessment	Provide a basis for evaluation of competence in relation to teaching standards	Best work in all content areas specified in standards	Photographs of bulletin board showing completed K-W-L* chart with caption explaining K-W-L procedure and how it connects to standards, lesson plans, class newsletter, assessment plans
Professional	Provide a basis for evaluation in relation to job or promotion requirements	Selected sample showing qualifications in relation to job requirements	Philosophy statement accompanied by evidence that demonstrates implementation of the philosophy; letter to parents, professional development certificates

Note: * K-W-L is "what I KNOW, what I WANT to know, and what I have LEARNED."

the relevance of evidence in terms of how well it helps you meet the purpose of the portfolio. Cognizance of your audience and the expectations they have can help you stay focused on the purpose. Table 7.2 summarizes portfolio types and purposes, and the nature of their respective evidence.

Each Piece of Evidence should be Weighed Against Criteria to Determine Best Fit

Portfolios are not about quantity. Each piece of evidence you select must do its part in telling your story—clearly demonstrating who you are, what you know, and what you can do in relation to the criteria you must meet. Matching evidence with criteria can be a painstaking process. It often requires you to sort through piles, boxes, and folders of saved items, all the while reflecting on what you are trying to say and show. It is a mindful, reflective process that has a strong impact on the quality of the finished product and the meaning you make of it. Criteria for a given portfolio may range from an open-ended guideline suggesting possible items for inclusion to a very prescriptive and comprehensive list of specific skills, knowledge and/or dispositions that you are required to demonstrate. No matter which criteria are in use, each piece of evidence must be very clearly connected to them.

Evidence must be Explained Clearly to Communicate Connections and Relevance to Criteria and/or Philosophy

Your reason for including each entry should be made transparent to the reader. Your purpose is to draw clear connections between the evidence and the specified criteria that form the backbone of the document. Whether in print or electronic format, each piece of evidence must be explained. The explanations serve to describe the context in which evidence was derived. It also lets the reader know how the evidence connects to a particular standard. The sample portfolio page (Figure 7.8) shows how explanations and artifacts work together to inform the reader.

The Body of Chosen Evidence should be Evaluated to Ensure Balanced Coverage of all Criteria

Although specifications for breadth and depth of coverage of criteria may vary, your task is to ensure that all criteria to which you are held are adequately addressed. Often portfolio builders have strengths in some areas and are more challenged in others. It is reasonable to expect that areas of strength might tend to be overrepresented, inadvertently leaving more difficult or less favored areas wanting. Keep your strengths, challenges, and preferences in mind as you develop, collect, and compile evidence. Remember that every

NAEYC Sub-Standard 4d. Building meaningful curriculum
Use own knowledge, and other resources to design, implement, & evaluate meaningful, challenging curriculum that promotes comprehensive developmental and learning outcomes for all young children.

Explanation
My infant/toddler curriculum focuses on exploration of the environment, relationships between caregivers and the children, and routines. These pictures focus on design & implementation of infant/toddler curriculum.

Cohl is exploring three bears. He is learning about texture and shape through his senses. He is also using his body to reach and balance and grasp the objects. He practicing eye-hand coordination. (Sitting out of camera range) I encourage him, cheer him on, and name what he is doing ("Oh, Cohl. You are really reaching for those bears. Look what you have – a blue bear"). This promotes language development.

Reflection
I realize more and more that curriculum with infants is about helping them become more competent & secure & providing them with interesting, safe activities that challenge them. They keep me thinking about what else I can do to promote their development.

FIGURE 7.8 Explanations and Artifacts Working Together

part of the criteria has its rightful place in the portfolio and needs to be addressed thoroughly in a convincing and meaningful manner.

Two strategies may prove useful to you in ensuring and examining coverage of the criteria: (1) create a filing system that allows you to sort and store evidence by criterion. This can help you avoid the problem of having an abundance in favored areas and little to none in less favored ones; (2) use a Portfolio Preparation Worksheet to inventory your evidence. A sample worksheet that we use with students who are working with the California state standards is given in Table 4.7 (p. 60). This tool is easily adapted to any criteria. It can be expanded to include subcategories or elements within each standard to accommodate more detailed inventorying.

Writing Rationales for Evidence Included in the Portfolio

In a course handout from the University of Florida (UFL) a rationale statement for portfolios is described in this way: "a professional argument for the evidence you are submitting to demonstrate the accomplished practice. The rationale statement communicates the link between the accomplished practice and the evidence. . . . If the reviewer of your portfolio has to construct the link on his/her own, then the . . . rationale statement is not strong enough." This statement contains several key ideas that we examine here more closely.

Providing a Professional Argument

It is incumbent upon professionals to be able to explain clearly, and sometimes defend, their practices, philosophies, and theoretical perspectives. Being well-versed in the professional knowledge base is, in fact, one of the criteria for being considered a professional. Being a professional also includes knowing what your theoretical perspective is and how your practice reflects it. The rationale points out to the reader how your practice embodies your beliefs and forwards your perspective. It draws from the knowledge base, providing support for your practice and lends credibility to your presentation.

Communicating the Link between Practice and Evidence

This is where the rubber meets the road. "Evidence" can look great, but say little. This is particularly true of photographs, but applies to all evidence. It is tempting to put in that cute, irresistible photo of the 3-year-old or the group of second graders, all with big toothy smiles. The value, however, of any evidence is in the information it conveys, whether it is an agenda you developed as part of a staff development program or a photo of children engaged in a math activity. Each piece of evidence must tell part of your story and unmistakably show what you know, how you have applied it, and why it matters in the overall scheme of your project or activity. Evidence must relate back to the standards in which you are demonstrating competence. When selecting evidence, ask yourself, "What does it tell the reader?", "Why have I included it?", and "How does it demonstrate my competence, knowledge, or accomplishment?" The reader should never be left with these questions on his or her mind.

Writing a Rationale Statement

Quoting again from the UFL handout ("What is a rationale," 2010): "A rationale begins with a description or summary of the artifact, provides an analysis of the essential elements of the artifact, and then provides a brief justification as to how the artifact demonstrates proficiency" in the corresponding standard or competency. It continues:

> The rationale is an argument . . . based on professional knowledge (i.e., literature, standards, personal practical knowledge). The rationale should discuss how and why your illustration [or artifact] exemplifies quality work connected to [the standard]. In other words, your rationale statement should show your reader that you understand the [standard], how you have chosen to illustrate

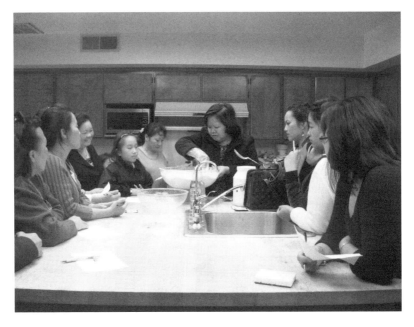

FIGURE 7.9 Vue Showing Moms How to Mix Dough

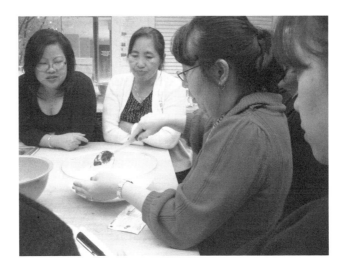

FIGURE 7.10 May Demonstrating Correct Dough Consistency

that understanding, and what the illustration demonstrates you are capable of doing.

We have provided several examples—one is a poorly developed rationale statement, the second example shows a well-developed statement.

FIGURE 7.11 Moms Trying Their Hand at Mixing the Dough

Evidence in Support of my Anti-Bias Curriculum Project

To help bring the family diversity into the classroom, the staff asked the families to share foods, traditions, and stories that were important to their families. The parents enjoyed coming together to cook and learn from each other, and to share their favorite family recipes with the children. Seeing the impact that the sharing had on the children, and families, the staff also decided to share their own stories and customs. This cooking experience is an example of one of the many activities that went on in the classroom and brought everyone closer together.

Notice that a lot of words are used, but very little information is actually conveyed. We know from the information that families and staff engaged in activities with a cultural theme, one of which was a cooking experience. That's about it. We have no context for understanding the importance of the activity or how it fits into the bigger picture or goal. We do not know if there is a sound reason to include such an activity, nor do we know how the activity connects to standards or how it demonstrates the student's mastery and application of knowledge. The reader is left asking questions such as "What was the scope of the activity?" "How does the literature support a practice such as this?" "How has the activity depicted here fostered cultural awareness, acceptance, and community?" "How does the artifact reflect, expand, promote your knowledge, skills, and/or dispositions?" "How does the artifact link knowledge and practice?"

Here is an example of a better rationale for the same photos.

The cooking activity shown in the photos depicts one of several experiences that brought family practices and foods into the classroom as part of my anti-bias curriculum project. My program has a variety of Southeast Asian families—Hmong, Thai, and Vietnamese—and Hispanic families. We also have bi-cultural Asian-Hispanic families who don't fit into just one cultural or ethnic group. Wardle (1996) and Derman-Sparks & Olsen Edwards (2010) point out that, besides helping children honor the groups to which they personally belong, we must also recognize and honor the differences within racial and cultural groups. We cannot define people by a category. Instead, we can explore our uniqueness and look at how our cultural heritage enriches and influences us.

In the photos, one of the Hmong moms shows the other mothers how to make rice cake, a traditional food that she makes regularly for her family. Some of the other Asian moms had never made it before from scratch. Instead, they buy it at the store. Some of the moms had never had it. I have included these photos because they represent a tool (cooking and sharing food) for increasing awareness of cultural and inner-cultural differences and similarities and building community. They also demonstrate my interest in the uniqueness of all of the members in my classroom community.

My anti-bias curriculum project demonstrates the knowledge I gained in the course on Working with Diverse Families. I became aware of the limitations of the traditional model of multicultural education which fails to recognize the tremendous diversity within cultural and ethnic groups and the way so many people see themselves that include, but go beyond, cultural associations. I also became aware that young children develop their identities more through their experiences as individuals than through their experiences as part of a cultural group (Cross, 1985).

This project demonstrates my understanding of Standard 2: Building Family and Community Relationships, specifically, element 2a: Knowing about and understanding diverse family and community characteristics, and 2b: Supporting and engaging families and communities through respectful, reciprocal relationships. Through feedback from the mothers, I learned that they gained a great deal of knowledge about each other and felt pride in sharing their favorite family foods. For some of the Asian moms, the experience brought back many childhood memories of their mothers making rice cake from scratch in their homes and the realization that they missed the experience because they didn't learn this skill. They also recognized that they wanted their children to know how to do this as a way of preserving something special from their culture. As a result of the project, the parents developed a closer bond with each other and have a greater sense of community and partnership.

Here is a recap of the criteria for writing rationales. They include:

- a description of the artifact,
- your reason for selecting the artifact from among the many you may have collected,
- your professional argument based on the literature for including artifact/s, and
- how the artifact demonstrates your understanding of and competence in a given standard.

A rationale can be written for each major artifact or group of like artifacts, such as photos depicting an activity or environment, a set of handouts developed for a workshop or parent meeting, a curriculum designed around a theme. They can also be written to encompass entire projects. Rationales will be handled differently depending upon the instructions you are given for your portfolio. Whether you write them for individual artifacts, for groups of like artifacts, or for whole projects, they must be descriptive, have a strong, professional basis, provide a clear link between the artifacts and your practice, and communicate your thorough knowledge and understanding of the standards.

Writing Captions that Accompany Artifacts or Illustrations

Captions accurately describe the who, what, where, when, and why of the photo or illustration. They provide far more detail than a label or title. Someone not looking at the picture or illustration, but hearing the caption read aloud, should be able to visualize what is depicted. We have provided several examples of captions to point out the differences between weak and strong captions.

Here is an example of a Poorly Developed Caption for Figure 7.12.

> During our construction project, I wanted the children to learn how structures are built. After observing and recording structures on the playground, I wanted them to build their own bridges.

Describing what you see in a photo or illustration, precisely and concisely, is the critical element involved in caption writing. In this example, the student has alluded to a construction project that deals with bridges in which the children were engaged. However, the only clues we have that the caption and the photo are related are that children are shown, one of whom is writing something on a tablet. The rest of the caption relates to the student's intentions (what she wanted the children to learn) and her goals for the children

FIGURE 7.12 Elyse Records What She Observes

(what she wanted them to do after they had recorded their observations). The photo can neither reveal her intentions, nor elucidate her goals We cannot *see* what is in her mind. The Well-Developed Caption shown in 7.12 explains precisely what the children are doing *and* relates their action to the project in which they are engaged. It provides not only context but details that are observable.

Here is an example of a Well-Developed Caption for Figure 7.12.

> As part of the bridge construction project in April 2010 at the Huggins Center, Elyse, with clipboard and pen in hand, draws a picture of a bridge she observes on the playground, while Sophie looks on.

Here is an example of a Poorly Developed Caption for Figure 7.13.

> It's important for young children to learn cooperation skills. Two preschoolers in this picture cooperate on an art project.

FIGURE 7.13 Two Preschoolers Taping Sticks Together

In this caption, the first sentence is a value statement. Although related to the theme of the photo (cooperation in action), it does not describe the action. The second sentence accurately indicates that two preschoolers are working together. However, it fails to provide detail as to their specific actions and how cooperation is in evidence.

Here is an example of a Well-Developed Caption for Figure 7.13.

> Marcus and Isabelle, both 3-year-olds at the Huggins Center, demonstrate cooperation. Isabelle holds a stick in place, while Marcus tapes it to the rest of their stick construction.

This is another example of a caption that provides the requisite information for the reader using unambiguous language. The description is precise and brief.

Characteristics of Portfolio Types that Influence Your Choices of Evidence

As described in Chapter 3, each type of portfolio has characteristics that make it distinct from the other types. These characteristics have ramifications for your choices of evidence. We will address each type of portfolio in turn and discuss implications for evidence in relation to the unique characteristics of each.

Developmental Portfolios

Developmental portfolios are most often seen in the context of classroom settings as course assignments or as part of participation grades. Adult developmental portfolios are most akin to the portfolios teachers use in classrooms to document children's growth and development. These portfolios are used as formative assessment tools that provide guidance to the teacher and adult learner with regard to learning needs. Adult developmental portfolios contain selected samples of evidence showing incremental learning and growth over a specified period of time. Developmental portfolios include, as a mainstay, works in progress and multiple drafts of the same assignment, as well as finished products. They are used by the instructor, in conjunction with the adult student, to assess progress and plan for continuing improvement. Of course, all of these are supported and tied together by reflections. In the case of developmental portfolios, the philosophy statement may be an element, but often as a work in progress.

Developmental portfolios are most often constructed using criteria that are idiosyncratic to a particular instructor or mentor. In some cases, criteria are negotiated or co-constructed with the portfolio builder. The tasks represented in developmental portfolios are designed to build or refine basic competencies in such things as observation, reflection, research, and planning. This prerequisite competency building is done concurrently with activities geared to expand and deepen content knowledge. The prerequisite knowledge, skills, and dispositions practiced and honed in the developmental portfolio are later employed by the portfolio builder to accomplish tasks and projects in order to demonstrate mastery of external criteria as required in showcase, professional, and assessment portfolios.

Examples from a Developmental Portfolio

The curriculum of the child development option for early care and education practitioners at our university is aligned with the National Association for the Education of Young Children (NAEYC) Standards for Programs. The most current version (2009) is shown in Table 7.3. Each course in the curriculum addresses one or more of the NAEYC standards. Developmental portfolios are used in some courses as a means for students to develop specific knowledge, skills, and dispositions that they will use in course projects and will later employ in the projects and products that will form their showcase portfolios.

The following example illustrates how Denise demonstrated, in her developmental portfolio, incremental progress in her ability to conduct detailed, descriptive, nonjudgmental observations of children. This skill was later applied in a case study in which detailed, serial observations of a particular child were used to demonstrate competency in NAEYC Standard 3—Observing, Documenting, and Assessing to Support Young Children and Families.

Table 7.3 National Association for the Education of Young Children Standards for Programs (2009)

National Association for the Education of Young Children
Standards for Programs (Revised 2009)

Standard 1. Promoting Child Development and Learning

Students prepared in early childhood degree programs are grounded in a child development knowledge base. They use their understanding of young children's characteristics and needs and of the multiple interacting influences on children's development and learning to create environments that are healthy, respectful, supportive, and challenging for each child.

Key elements of Standard 1
1a: Knowing and understanding young children's characteristics and needs
1b: Knowing and understanding the multiple influences on development and learning
1c: Using developmental knowledge to create healthy, respectful, supportive, and challenging learning environments

Standard 2. Building Family and Community Relationships

Students prepared in early childhood degree programs understand that successful early childhood education depends upon partnerships with children's families and communities. They know about, understand, and value the importance and complex characteristics of children's families and communities. They use this understanding to create respectful, reciprocal relationships that support and empower families and to involve all families in their children's development and learning.

Key elements of Standard 2
2a: Knowing about and understanding diverse family and community characteristics
2b: Supporting and engaging families and communities through respectful, reciprocal relationships
2c: Involving families and communities in their children's development and learning

Standard 3. Observing, Documenting, and Assessing to Support Young Children and Families

Students prepared in early childhood degree programs understand that child observation, documentation, and other forms of assessment are central to the practice of all early childhood professionals. They know about and understand the goals, benefits, and uses of assessment. They know about and use systematic observations, documentation, and other effective assessment strategies in a responsible way, in partnership with families and other professionals, to positively influence the development of every child.

Key elements of Standard 3
3a: Understanding the goals, benefits, and uses of assessment
3b: Knowing about assessment partnerships with families and with professional colleagues
3c: Knowing about and using observation, documentation, and other appropriate assessment tools and approaches
3d: Understanding and practicing responsible assessment to promote positive outcomes for each child

Standard 4. Using Developmentally Effective Approaches to Connect with Children and Families

Students prepared in early childhood degree programs understand that teaching and learning with young children is a complex enterprise, and its details vary depending on children's ages, characteristics, and the settings within which teaching and learning occur. They understand and use positive relationships and supportive

Table 7.3 Continued

interactions as the foundation for their work with young children and families. Students know, understand, and use a wide array of developmentally appropriate approaches, instructional strategies, and tools to connect with children and families and positively influence each child's development and learning.

Key elements of Standard 4
4a: Understanding positive relationships and supportive interactions as the founda-
     tion of their work with children
4b: Knowing and understanding effective strategies and tools for early education
4c: Using a broad repertoire of developmentally appropriate teaching/learning
     approaches
4d: Reflecting on their own practice to promote positive outcomes for each child

Standard 5. Using Content Knowledge to Build Meaningful Curriculum
Students prepared in early childhood degree programs use their knowledge of academic disciplines to design, implement, and evaluate experiences that promote positive development and learning for each and every young child. Students understand
the importance of developmental domains and academic (or content) disciplines in
an early childhood curriculum. They know the essential concepts, inquiry tools, and
structure of content areas, including academic subjects, and can identify resources to
deepen their understanding. Students use their own knowledge and other resources
to design, implement, and evaluate meaningful, challenging curricula that promote
comprehensive developmental and learning outcomes for every young child.

Key elements of Standard 5
5a: Understanding content knowledge and resources in academic disciplines
5b: Knowing and using the central concepts, inquiry tools, and structures of content
     areas or academic disciplines
5c: Using their own knowledge, appropriate early learning standards, and other
     resources to design, implement, and evaluate meaningful, challenging curricula
     for each child

Standard 6. Becoming a Professional
Students prepared in early childhood degree programs identify and conduct themselves as members of the early childhood profession. They know and use ethical
guidelines and other professional standards related to early childhood practice. They
are continuous, collaborative learners who demonstrate knowledgeable, reflective,
and critical perspectives on their work, making informed decisions that integrate
knowledge from a variety of sources. They are informed advocates for sound educational practices and policies.

Key elements of Standard 6
6a: Identifying and involving oneself with the early childhood field
6b: Knowing about and upholding ethical standards and other professional guidelines
6c: Engaging in continuous, collaborative learning to inform practice
6d: Integrating knowledgeable, reflective, and critical perspectives on early education
6e: Engaging in informed advocacy for children and the profession

Denise

The guidelines for Denise's developmental portfolio required that she conduct at least five hours of observation of preschool children at play over the
course of five weeks. In preparation for this, she and her fellow students were
instructed in how to write running records. They explored the differences among
description, interpretation, and judgment, and engaged in guided practice

using video clips and follow-up discussion. In class each week, the students reviewed each other's observations using a rubric. With the instructor, the group explored, questioned, and clarified their work with a focus on how they could improve their observation technique. Table 7.4 shows excerpts from

TABLE 7.4 Excerpts of Observations and Feedback

Observation #1	Feedback
. . . Sarah looks for another toy. She gets bored so she doesn't stay with any activity or toy very long before moving to something that appears to be more interesting. Sarah picks up a stacking toy that Joshua definitely wants and he takes it from her. Sarah becomes upset and starts to cry. The teacher makes him give the toy back and tells him he must share . . .	Remember to describe the actions of the children without interpreting their motives or feelings. Describe the behavior and/or body language/facial expressions that gave you the impression that she was bored or that the toy appeared more interesting, but don't assume how she feels. What behavior made you think Joshua definitely wanted the toy? Maybe it wasn't about the toy. Maybe he wanted Sarah's attention. Can you know this, or is it a guess? Stick to what you see, not to what you think happened.

Observation #5	Feedback
Angie and Marcie were in the dramatic play area. Angie said to Marcie, "You sit here. You be the one to eat and I will make lunch." She handed Marcie a child-produced book about foods and said, "What do you want for lunch?" Marcie opened the book and pointed to a picture of spaghetti. She said, "Do you have this?" Angie answered, "Yes we do." She turned quickly and skipped to the sink. She took out a plastic carrot and cauliflower. She put them on a plate and walked slowly back to the table, carefully balancing the vegetables. She put the plate on the table in front of Marcie. Marcie looked down at the plate and frowned. Then she looked up at Angie with a half-smile on her face. She said in a loud voice, "That's NOT spaghetti." Angie answered, "It's the only spaghetti we have." Marcie replied, "I don't like that kind. I want pizza." Angie said firmly, "You can't have something else until you eat this." Marcie pushed away from the table, stood up, and with her hands on her hips, said, "I'm going to another restaurant."	Good use of descriptive words. You conveyed the action without interpreting their feelings or intentions. I could really see the play unfold. You captured the children's dialogue very well. You let their words and expressions tell the story.

Denise's observations and feedback she received from her peers and instructor. This example illustrates the progression of Denise's work on observations.

In the reflection following her fifth observation, she wrote,

> This is definitely getting easier. I don't feel like I have to write down every single thing in order to capture what is happening. I'm really keeping in mind description, description, description! I've gotten much better about not assuming what the children are thinking or intending. I'm focusing on really seeing what they're doing. Now, I'm paying much closer attention to my feelings about what I see vs. what I see and knowing the difference. I can't imagine teaching now without observing.

At the end of the five-week period, Denise compiled her observation work samples and reflections for her developmental portfolio. When taken as a whole, the evidence showed clear proof of growth in her observation skills. Her reflections documented the evolution of her thinking about observation as it relates to her and as it relates to teaching. In her final reflection on the observation experiences, she made connections between where she had come from (in terms of using this skill), what she could do now, and how this skill would contribute to her practice in the future.

> I thought I really understood observation before I started this process. Now I see how much I missed before and how much I assumed about what was happening without realizing it. This is much harder than it looks. Now when I observe the children, I keep asking myself, "What am I really seeing—and what do I think I'm seeing?" Now I know the difference and I know the questions to ask myself. I think being a better observer will make me a better teacher because this is really helping me not label the children. Now, I'm trying harder to understand them and how what's going on around them affects them. I've realized that sometimes play problems I think the children have are really the result of the dysfunction of the classroom or lack of staff being in tune with the needs of the children. I know now that I must make time in my everyday practice to observe the children and document what I see. This experience has shown me how useful observation is as a teaching tool.

Developmental Portfolios as Preparation for Showcase or Assessment Portfolios

As we pointed out above, developmental portfolios often constitute preparatory work. They focus on acquisition and refinement of knowledge, skills, and dispositions that students will later employ as they set about the work of demonstrating competencies. Figure 7.14 provides an example of the relationships between a developmental portfolio, a showcase

Developmental Portfolio: Competency-building tasks	Showcase Portfolio: Denise's portfolio entry outline	NAEYC Standards
Observe preschoolers using specimen & running record methods. Conduct a series of 5 30-minute field observations on play behaviors in young children. Record your observations with attention to completeness, objectivity, specificity, mood, and directness (Curtis & Carter, 2000). **Analyze** play behaviors using specified theoretical perspectives. **Reflect** on each observation experience noting where you started in your skill & understanding of observation, what you learned about yourself and your practice through the observation experience, how you will use your learning in future practice.	**Case study of Marissa:** • Assessing play problems & supporting play entry and prosocial play skills • Standards this project addresses & how it does so. • Major learning achieved through execution of the project Evidence that demonstrates competencies: **Personal documents** Reflections, narrative re: connection to philosophy **Artifacts** Observations, assessment of child's play behaviors, summaries of planning & follow-up meetings with co-teachers, report from parent conference, video clips of Marissa playing with peers, intervention strategies to support play entry and prosocial play skills, assessment of strategy outcomes and report of future plans. How each artifact illustrates learning & demonstrates competency	**Standard 3. Observing, Documenting, and Assessing to Support Young Children and Families** Know about and understand the goals, benefits, and uses of assessment. Know about and use systematic observations, documentation, and other effective assessment strategies in a responsible way, in partnership with families and other professionals, to positively influence children's development and learning. **Standard 4. Teaching and Learning** Students prepared in early childhood degree programs understand that teaching and learning with young children is a complex enterprise, and its details vary depending on children's ages, characteristics, and the settings within which teaching and learning occur. They understand and use positive relationships and supportive interactions as the foundation for their work with young children and families. Students know, understand, and use a wide array of developmentally appropriate approaches, instructional strategies, and tools to connect with children and families and positively influence each child's development and learning. 4a: Understanding positive relationships and supportive interactions as the foundation of their work with children

FIGURE 7.14 Relationships between a Developmental Portfolio, a Showcase Portfolio, and Criteria

portfolio, and criteria. The first column—Developmental Portfolio—summarizes a set of competency-building tasks (shown in bold) that students practiced as part of their developmental portfolios: observation, analysis, and reflection. These skills, once mastered, were available to students as they designed and implemented their showcase portfolio projects. Column 2—Showcase Portfolio—shows the outline that Denise used to plan and execute her case study of Marissa. Each of the skills that she refined through the developmental portfolio was employed, and resulted in evidence, in her comprehensive project in the showcase portfolio: observation, analysis, and reflection (also shown in bold). The third column—NAEYC Standards—identifies the specific standards addressed in the portfolio entry in which the skills observation, analysis, and reflection are embedded.

Showcase Portfolios

Showcase portfolios, like their developmental cousins, are somewhat idiosyncratic. Their criteria are often formulated at the program level rather than being designed by an instructor. These portfolios often constitute part of a graduation requirement internal to the institution conferring the degree or certificate. Although external standards, such as those promulgated by professional associations, frequently provide the framework for this type of portfolio, these entities have no evaluative function with respect to the institution in this regard. For instance, the degree option for practitioners, mentioned above, uses NAEYC's Standards for Programs (2009) as the criteria for students' showcase portfolios. Whereas teacher credential candidates' assessment portfolios (addressed later in this section) require coverage of each element within each state standard, showcase portfolios, as we use them, are comprised of up to six comprehensive projects. Each of these projects integrates and reflects multiple, broadly defined national standards. Showcase portfolio builders exercise a high degree of autonomy in determining portfolio content. As these students are all working professionals in early care and education, their projects correspond directly to the needs and demands of their work environments and professional interests and development.

Figures 7.15 through 7.18 depict a project from Kathryn's showcase portfolio. She developed a comprehensive curriculum project that she implemented with her preschool group and their families—all residents of a small, rural

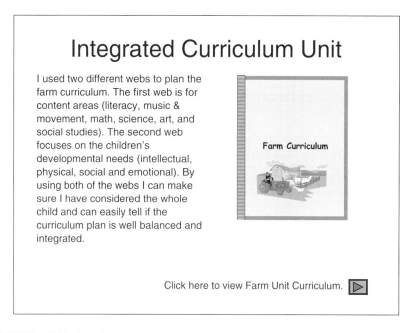

FIGURE 7.15 Kathryn's Integrated Farm Unit

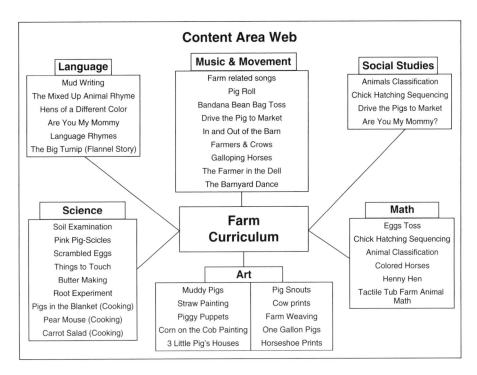

FIGURE 7.16 Kathryn's Content Area Web

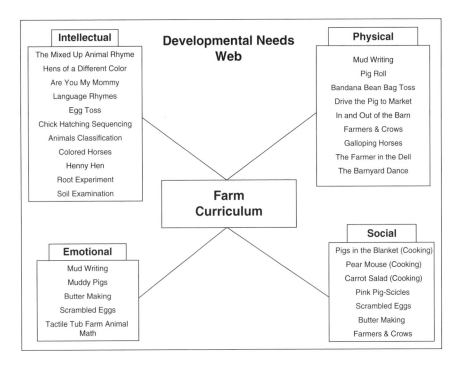

FIGURE 7.17 Kathryn's Development Needs Web

FIGURE 7.18 Kathryn's Parent Night Presentation

town in the heart of farm country in California's Central Valley. Kathryn's curriculum project had four dimensions: (1) the development of integrated, topically and culturally relevant curriculum for 4-year-olds in her classroom; (2) staff development for the staff in her center; (3) parent education on developmentally appropriate curriculum and play in the classroom; and (4) parent involvement. The standards she addressed in her project are shown in Table 7.5.

Kathryn addressed Standard 2 by selecting as the basis for her curriculum unit the farm-life experiences of the children and families with whom she works. By doing so, she validated their experience as a valuable subject worthy of investigation in the classroom. She invited the parents to participate in a variety of ways throughout the implementation of the unit. Kathryn demonstrated competence in Standard 4, particularly 4b and 4d, through her inclusion of numerous teaching strategies, activities, and tools that spanned and connected developmental domains and content areas. Kathryn planned, implemented, and evaluated two activities that focused on Standard 5: an in-service training for the center staff on integrated curriculum, and a presentation for parents. Both of these activities explained and promoted developmentally appropriate curriculum and play in the classroom. Notice the small icons on the bottom right corners of Figures 7.15 and 7.18. Kathryn prepared her portfolio in electronic format using PowerPoint presentation software. The icons link to additional sources of evidence that explain and support her project. Electronic portfolios will be discussed in Chapter 8.

We showed in the previous section how developmental portfolios are used to build foundational knowledge, skills, and dispositions that can later be

Table 7.5 Standards Addressed in Kathryn's Curriculum Project

Standard 2. Building Family and Community Relationships

Students prepared in early childhood degree programs understand that successful early childhood education depends upon partnerships with children's families and communities. They know about, understand, and value the importance and complex characteristics of children's families and communities. They use this understanding to create respectful, reciprocal relationships that support and empower families and to involve all families in their children's development and learning.

2c: Involving families and communities in their children's development and learning

Standard 4. Using Developmentally Effective Approaches to Connect with Children and Families

Students prepared in early childhood degree programs understand that teaching and learning with young children is a complex enterprise, and its details vary depending on children's ages, characteristics, and the settings within which teaching and learning occur. They understand and use positive relationships and supportive interactions as the foundation for their work with young children and families. Students know, understand, and use a wide array of developmentally appropriate approaches, instructional strategies, and tools to connect with children and families and positively influence each child's development and learning.

4c: Using a broad repertoire of developmentally appropriate teaching/learning approaches

Standard 5. Using Content Knowledge to Build Meaningful Curriculum

Students prepared in early childhood degree programs use their knowledge of academic disciplines to design, implement, and evaluate experiences that promote positive development and learning for each and every young child. Students understand the importance of developmental domains and academic (or content) disciplines in an early childhood curriculum. They know the essential concepts, inquiry tools, and structure of content areas, including academic subjects, and can identify resources to deepen their understanding. Students use their own knowledge and other resources to design, implement, and evaluate meaningful, challenging curricula that promote comprehensive developmental and learning outcomes for every young child.

5c: Using their own knowledge, appropriate early learning standards, and other resources to design, implement, and evaluate meaningful, challenging curricula for each child.

Standard 6. Becoming a Professional

Students prepared in early childhood degree programs identify and conduct themselves as members of the early childhood profession. They know and use ethical guidelines and other professional standards related to early childhood practice. They are continuous, collaborative learners who demonstrate knowledgeable, reflective, and critical perspectives on their work, making informed decisions that integrate knowledge from a variety of sources. They are informed advocates for sound educational practices and policies.

6c: Engaging in continuous, collaborative learning to inform practice

6d: Integrating knowledgeable, reflective, and critical perspectives on early education

---

used in showcase portfolios. Developmental portfolios are not limited, however, to this use. They can be employed as proficiency-building devices in any learning context.

The showcase portfolio is an effective communication tool, particularly when the display of multifaceted projects is the goal. Now, we turn to portfolios used for evaluation purposes. You will recall from Chapter 3 that there are two types of portfolios used for evaluation: assessment and professional.

Assessment Portfolios

Assessment portfolios are most commonly used in academic settings, particularly those that involve teacher credentialing and other types of specialized preparation. They are also used to obtain national teacher certification. Criteria that govern assessment portfolios vary by source (e.g., national professional associations, state licensing agencies). Criteria can be very broad or highly specific. In any case, assessment portfolios are intended to show competence in all areas specified in the criteria to which they are subject.

We have included a brief discussion of criteria related to teacher credentialing and other specialized preparation in order to draw the differences between them as they affect portfolios. Being knowledgeable about the criteria, or levels of criteria, to which you will be held accountable is a crucial step in portfolio success. That knowledge will guide you in your selection of evidence and prepare you for its eventual assessment. As a starting point, we have provided an overview in Table 7.6 of the standards and the categories of professional preparation to which they connect.

Having a sense of the relationships among various sets of standards can be helpful when trying to translate criteria into action plans that are then reflected in your portfolio. Keep in mind that the standards to which you will be held are determined by your institution and the political landscape of your state or region.

Now to the standards. National accrediting bodies, such as the National Council for Accreditation of Teacher Education (NCATE) and the National Association for the Education of Young Children (NAEYC) have come to be seen in education as the standard-bearers of quality. These bodies accredit teacher preparation and advanced programs in higher education. The standards set by such bodies directly influence the content of assessment

Table 7.6 Categories of Professional Preparation and Sets of Standards

	NCATE	NAEYC Core Standards	NAEYC Advanced Standards	State Teaching Credential Standards
Initial teacher credentialing with accreditation in early childhood education (K–3)	yes	yes	no	yes
Advanced preparation (specialist, Master's in early childhood education)	yes	yes	yes	no

portfolios in accredited programs. Not all of these programs are accredited, nor do all accredited programs require portfolios.

The NCATE standard shown in Table 7.7 is an example of criteria that pertain specifically and directly to teacher candidate and advanced preparation. It relates directly to candidate performance criteria and provides guidance as to portfolio content.

In addition to being an accrediting body in its own right, the NAEYC is a specialty professional association (SPA) recognized by NCATE as the body that defines the standards for early childhood education. Teacher preparation programs with a K-3 emphasis that are NCATE/NAEYC accredited adhere to both NCATE standards and NAEYC core standards for initial licensure of teachers. The NAEYC core standards were shown in Table 7.3.

Accredited institutions that grant advanced certificates and degrees in early childhood education adhere to NCATE standards, and both the core and advanced standards set by NAEYC. "[A]t the advanced level, candidates demonstrate competence at a higher level and with greater depth and specialization" (Hyson, 2003, p. 76). These candidates do not address state teaching credential standards but are "expected to hold an initial license in early childhood education or a closely related field" (Hyson, 2003, p. 76). The NAEYC advanced standards are shown in Table 7.8.

In addition to these national accreditation standards, teacher-preparation programs are subject to requirements specified by their individual state agencies responsible for teacher credentialing. This does not necessarily apply to advanced preparation programs. Although NCATE and NAEYC standards are well aligned with each other, state standards are not always as well aligned with those at the national level. The California Standards for the Teaching Profession, Table 7.9, are a case in point. The national standards contain elements specific to the education of young children, ethics, and advocacy, whereas the California state standards do not.

At the institutional level, teacher-preparation programs, in conjunction with their respective states, define how they will meet their state requirements for assessment of teacher candidates. The institution may determine that it will use portfolios as one method to assess student learning. This is the case at our

Table 7.7 National Council for Accreditation of Teacher Education I: Candidate Performance

NCATE I. Candidate Performance
Standard 1: Candidate Knowledge, Skills, and Dispositions
Candidates preparing to work in schools as teachers or other professional school personnel know and demonstrate the content, pedagogical, and professional knowledge, skills, and dispositions necessary to help all students learn. Assessments indicate that candidates meet professional, state, and institutional standards.

Table 7.8 National Association for the Education of Young Children Advanced Standards

NAEYC ADVANCED STANDARDS

I. CORE STANDARDS (shown on Table 7.3, pages 113–114)

II. ESSENTIAL PROFESSIONAL TOOLS FOR ALL CANDIDATES IN ADVANCED PROGRAMS.

1. **Cultural Competence:** Advanced program candidates demonstrate a high level of competence in understanding and responding to diversity of culture, language, and ethnicity.

2. **Knowledge and Application of Ethical Principles:** Advanced program candidates demonstrate in-depth knowledge and thoughtful application of NAEYC's Code of Ethical Conduct and other guidelines relevant to their professional role.

3. **Communication Skills:** Advanced program candidates possess a high level of oral, written, and technological communication skills, with specialization for the specific professional roles(s) emphasized in the program.

4. **Mastery of Relevant Theory and Research:** Advanced program candidates demonstrate in-depth, critical knowledge of the theory and research relevant to the professional role(s) and focus area(s) emphasized in the program.

5. **Skills in Identifying and Using Professional Resources:** Advanced program candidates demonstrate a high level of skill in identifying and using the human, material, and technological resources needed to perform their professional roles and to keep abreast of the field's changing knowledge base.

6. **Inquiry Skills and Knowledge of Research Methods:** Using systematic and professionally accepted approaches, Advanced program candidates demonstrate inquiry skills, showing their ability to investigate questions relevant to their practice and professional goals.

7. **Skills in Collaborating, Teaching, and Mentoring:** Advanced program candidates demonstrate the flexible, varied skills needed to work collaboratively and effectively with other adults in professional roles.

8. **Advocacy Skills:** Advanced program candidates demonstrate competence in articulation and advocating for sound professional practices and public policies for the positive development and learning of all young children.

9. **Leadership Skills:** Advanced program candidates reflect on and use their abilities and opportunities to think strategically, build consensus, create change, and influence better outcomes for children, families, and the profession.

III. ADDITIONAL SPECIALIZED COMPETENCIES

Beyond the core standards and essential professional tools, programs may identify additional competencies essential to particular focus areas or specializations. Examples might be knowledge of the legislative process for candidates specializing in public policy and advocacy, or skills in personnel and fiscal management for candidates in an early childhood administration program. Programs with such additional competencies should identify them in clear performance language and include criteria by which the program assesses these competencies.   (Hyson, 2003, p. 77)

Table 7.9 California Standards for the Teaching Profession 2009

STANDARD ONE ENGAGING AND SUPPORTING ALL STUDENTS IN LEARNING	STANDARD TWO CREATING AND MAINTAINING EFFECTIVE ENVIRONMENTS FOR STUDENT LEARNING
1.1 Using knowledge of students to engage them in learning 1.2 Connecting learning to students' prior knowledge, backgrounds, life experiences, and interests 1.3 Connecting subject matter to meaningful, real-life contexts 1.4 Using a variety of instructional strategies, resources, and technologies to meet students' diverse learning needs 1.5 Promoting critical thinking through inquiry, problem solving, and reflection 1.6 Monitoring student learning and adjusting instruction while teaching	2.1 Promoting social development and responsibility within a caring community where each student is treated fairly and respectfully 2.2 Creating physical or virtual learning environments that promote student learning, reflect diversity, and encourage constructive and productive interactions among students 2.3 Establishing and maintaining learning environments that are physically, intellectually, and emotionally safe 2.4 Creating a rigorous learning environment with high expectations and appropriate support for all students 2.5 Developing, communicating, and maintaining high standards for individual and group behavior 2.6 Employing classroom routines, procedures, norms, and supports for positive behavior to ensure a climate in which all students can learn 2.7 Using instructional time to optimize learning
STANDARD THREE UNDERSTANDING AND ORGANIZING SUBJECT MATTER FOR STUDENT LEARNING	STANDARD FOUR PLANNING INSTRUCTION AND DESIGNING LEARNING EXPERIENCES FOR ALL STUDENTS
3.1 Demonstrating knowledge of subject matter, academic content standards, and curriculum frameworks 3.2 Applying knowledge of student development and proficiencies to ensure student understanding of subject matter	4.1 Using knowledge of students' academic readiness, language proficiency, cultural background, and individual development to plan instruction 4.2 Establishing and articulating goals for student learning

3.3 Organizing curriculum to facilitate student understanding of the subject matter

3.4 Utilizing instructional strategies that are appropriate to the subject matter

3.5 Using and adapting resources, technologies, and standards-aligned instructional materials, including adopted materials, to make subject matter accessible to all students

3.6 Addressing the needs of English learners and students with special needs to provide equitable access to the content

4.3 Developing and sequencing long-term and short-term instructional plans to support student learning

4.4 Planning instruction that incorporates appropriate strategies to meet the learning needs of all students

4.5 Adapting instructional plans and curricular materials to meet the assessed learning needs of all students

STANDARD FIVE ASSESSING STUDENTS FOR LEARNING	STANDARD SIX DEVELOPING AS A PROFESSIONAL EDUCATOR
5.1 Applying knowledge of the purposes, characteristics, and uses of different types of assessments	6.1 Reflecting on teaching practice in support of student learning
5.2 Collecting and analyzing assessment data from a variety of sources to inform instruction	6.2 Establishing professional goals and engaging in continuous and purposeful professional growth and development
5.3 Reviewing data, both individually and with colleagues, to monitor student learning	6.3 Collaborating with colleagues and the broader professional community to support teacher and student learning
5.4 Using assessment data to establish learning goals and to plan, differentiate, and modify instruction	6.4 Working with families to support student learning
5.5 Involving all students in self-assessment, goal setting, and monitoring progress	6.5 Engaging local communities in support of the instructional program
5.6 Using available technologies to assist in assessment, analysis, and communication of student learning	6.6 Managing professional responsibilities to maintain motivation and commitment to all students
5.7 Using assessment information to share timely and comprehensible feedback with students and their families	6.7 Demonstrating professional responsibility, integrity, and ethical conduct

university. Some programs within the teacher-education program use portfolios to assess student learning and readiness for the teaching profession.

In the sections that follow are examples from portfolios fitting the two categories of standards: those that tend to be broad (national standards) and those that are very specific, such as the state standards found in California.

Knowing the standards that govern your portfolio will enable you to use these examples to best advantage.

Assessment Portfolios for Initial Teaching Credential

The students in our early childhood credential program prepare a portfolio that is organized around California's six standards for the teaching profession. The process of building an assessment portfolio based on these standards prepares students to do what is expected of them as new teachers in the California public schools. The content for these initial portfolios is highly prescriptive; students must document competence for all of the standards and elements of the standards. We have included a variety of samples from portfolios that illustrate how students have documented their competence in initial licensure standards.

Laurel's Portfolio

Laurel used artifacts from her student teaching experience to document her competence in Standard 1.1—Connecting student's prior knowledge, life experiences, and interests with learning goals. To document competence in this element, Laurel used a copy of a third-grade student's written work in which he described his prior experiences with teeth as part of a unit on dental health (Figure 7.19). The writing activity helped the student connect his prior

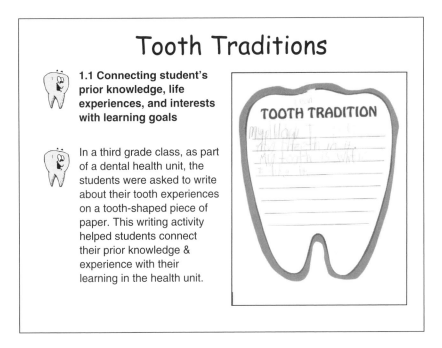

FIGURE 7.19 Tooth Traditions

knowledge and real-life experiences with teeth to his new learning in the health unit. The content of the health unit also provided a focus for working on writing skills.

The Tooth Traditions artifact documents the connection between a specific element of the standard and the classroom activity that Laurel designed and implemented with the children to demonstrate her competency. Laurel used a series of artifacts to document her work in relation to the various elements of this standard. After assembling the artifacts, Laurel wrote the following reflection. The reflection—a personal document—is part of the evidence that illustrates her growth as a professional as it relates to this standard.

Laurel's Reflection

Engaging and Supporting All Students in Learning Where I Started

I started out believing that this was an easy standard to achieve, that engagement was just students paying attention and that supporting was monitoring. I thought this standard would be met if students were looking at me and I was looking back.

Where I Am Now

I now know that much more is needed in order for this standard to be met. Engagement is active involvement in meaningful activities or curriculum. In order to engage and support all students in the learning process one must connect to their prior knowledge, use a variety of strategies in order to meet the needs of all students, and provide activities that make subject matter meaningful. Having the students' attention is not enough.

Where I'm Going

I feel that I have come a long way in this area, but realize there is still more to learn. I plan to develop in this area by attending in-service sessions, staff development workshops, and through the help of my BTSA [Beginning Teacher Support and Assessment] support provider and school staff.

Laurel's reflection conveys her personal gains from having done the set of activities related to Standard 1, of which Tooth Traditions was a part. At the same time, the act of writing reflections demonstrates competence in Standard 6.1—Reflecting on teaching practice and planning professional development.

Elsewhere in her portfolio, Laurel used personal documents as sources of evidence to show competence in Standard 6.2—Establishing professional goals and pursing opportunities to grow professionally. One example was a certificate of participation for helping to plan, organize, and present a session at a local conference (Figure 7.20).

Standard Six:
Developing as a Professional Educator

6.2 Establishing professional goals and pursuing opportunities to grow professionally.

Certificate of participation for helping to plan, organize, and present the session: "Ethical Dilemmas! What's that got to do with teaching?"

FIGURE 7.20 Personal Document: Certificate of Participation

Assessment Portfolios for Advanced Candidates

Assessment portfolios for advanced candidates meet NCATE standards and NAEYC core and advanced standards. Students meeting these standards generally have more autonomy with regard to portfolio development than do teacher credentialing candidates in that they are guided by national standards, which are more open-ended and less prescriptive than some states' requirements. The examples we have included from portfolios of candidates in advanced programs serve to demonstrate how broad standards can be addressed.

The table of contents shown in Table 7.10 is from the portfolio of Lori, a preschool teacher and Master's student. She developed the portfolio as part of her supervised fieldwork placement the semester before doing her final Master's project or thesis. Lori's table of contents reflects her flexible, creative approach to the broad national standards. Note the item "My Philosophy in Action." This is an item of Lori's own invention.

Lori used "My Philosophy in Action" to illustrate clearly how her philosophy guides her teaching. Her artifacts, which include scanned images of children's written work and parents' notations on the work, corroborate her philosophy (Interactive Journal: home–school collaboration, Figure 7.21). With regard to these journals, she wrote, "Parents scaffold the children's developing writing by translating their beginning writing into standard writing for the teacher. Children read their entries to the teacher upon returning to school."

Table 7.10 Example of Table of Contents

Through this evidence, Lori provided documentation for a variety of standards.

- NAEYC Standard 2—Building family and community relations.
- NAEYC Standard 4—Teaching and learning.
- NAEYC Essential Professional Tool 7—Skills in collaborating, teaching, and mentoring.

By meeting these NAEYC standards, Lori simultaneously provided documentation for her work in NCATE's Standard 1. The Interactive Journals became a medium through which Lori involved parents in the school life of their children. It validated the parents as the children's first teachers.

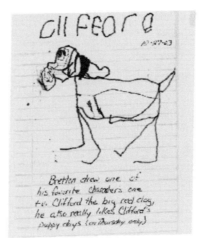

Sample of Interactive Journals: A home-school collaboration

- Parents scaffold the children's developing writing by translating their beginning writing into standard writing for the teacher. Children read their entries to the teacher upon returning to school.

FIGURE 7.21 Interactive Journal: Home–School Collaboration

It created a meaningful collaboration between the parents and teacher, promoted ongoing dialogue between home and school, and allowed children to see that their parents value education. At the same time, the activity helped the children develop literacy skills and creative expression. It also provided an opportunity for children to work with their parents on a meaningful task.

Sometimes artifacts are construed as only those things that relate to, or depict, children's activities. The Interactive Journal example used above is that kind of artifact. Artifacts are also those items that the portfolio builder uses to conduct the business of their own learning, however, such as field experience logs. Table 7.11 is an excerpt from a field experience log that another Master's student, Brenda, included in her portfolio.

In addition to artifacts, personal documents constitute evidence of fulfillment of criteria. Brenda's Personal Growth Plan provides such evidence. Figure 7.22 shows the introduction to the plan that Brenda included in her electronic portfolio. Within the introduction, Brenda embedded links that take the reader to the actual Personal Growth Plan. Chapter 8 will cover electronic portfolios.

Brenda's Personal Growth Plan documents progress toward meeting NAEYC Standard 5—Growing as a Professional. In developing her plan, she had to consider steps she would need to take to continue her professional growth. This began with a self-assessment of her beliefs in light of exemplary

Table 7.11 Brenda's Field Experience Log

Date	Hours	Site	Age/Grade	Participation/Observation
2/17/04	12:00–3:00 pm (3 hrs)	Sunset	5–8 year olds K-3	Participation in "Girls Grow Strong" in Girl Scouting! Learning about "Healthy Moves" and expressing feelings. Songs and games. (NAEYC Exceptional Professional Tools 7) (EPT 7)
2/12/04	12:00–3:00 pm (3 hrs)	Sunset	5–8 year olds K-3	Showing respect for others means treating them the way you want to be treated. Meeting people. Different eating customs, song and games, and the Promise and Law. (NAEYC EPT 1, 2)
2/18/04	12:00–3:00 pm (3 hrs)	Del Mar	5–8 year olds K-3	Participation in activity singing, stretch arms and legs by touching the ground. Observed monitoring staff interaction with the children. (NAEYC Standard 5)
2/24/04	12:00–3:00 pm (3 hrs)	Sunset	5–8 year olds K-3	Model hygiene routines for girls—washing hands and combing hair. Songs and games—Tarzana and Great Big Moose (NAEYC Standard 1)

practices in early childhood education. She then identified an area of special interest to pursue. Her final step in developing the plan was to identify her short- and long-term goals, create a timeline, and select readings applicable to her area of interest.

As you can see from this overview, assessment portfolios accommodate a wide variety of standards with varying degrees of prescription. They are the most common type used for evaluation, but not the only type. Professional portfolios are also used for evaluative purposes. We will discuss two types of professional portfolios in the next sections: those that are used for job seeking and those that are used when seeking promotion.

Professional Portfolios

Professional portfolios are primarily used in employment contexts: when applying for a position or seeking promotion. The content of professional portfolios reflects the requirements set out by employers, just as developmental,

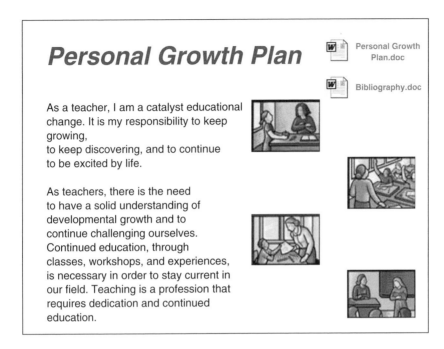

FIGURE 7.22 Brenda's Personal Growth Plan Introduction

showcase, or assessment portfolios reflect requirements set out by their guiding authorities: an instructor, an institution, a state credentialing body, or a professional association. Unlike other types, however, professional portfolios often contain items not particularly specified by employers, but which are nonetheless informative.

Portfolios used for Job Seeking

The professional portfolio is one of several tools employers might use to determine the best fit for a given position. Sometimes they are used as a pre-screening device. They can also be used as a visual aid in an interview session. It can be assumed that employers in educational settings, as a rule, would expect a portfolio to contain, at a minimum, a résumé, a philosophy statement, and letters of reference. Beyond these items, employers vary in their expectations. Job descriptions often provide excellent guidance as to what to include in the portfolio. Employers' websites or print materials are also good sources of information for portfolio planning. They may give you insights into employment culture/policies/programs to which you might decide to address a portion of your portfolio content.

In building a professional portfolio for interview purposes, put yourself in the place of the employer. Consider what you would want to know about an applicant that would help you make a good hiring decision. At the same time, consider the length of the document. Your goal is to present your background convincingly yet concisely. We recommend including the following sections and items.

1. *Cover Page*
2. *Table of Contents*
3. *Professional Background*: This section of the portfolio includes personal documents that describe who you are professionally. Take care in considering how much to include. The quality and substance of the documentation, from the standpoint of the reader, is important to keep in mind. We think the essentials include:

   ■ your philosophy statement,
   ■ current résumé,
   ■ permits, licenses, certificates, and/or clearances,
   ■ letters of recommendation,
   ■ unofficial, but complete, transcripts,
   ■ professional growth plan,
   ■ awards and certificates related to professional development and service, and
   ■ anything else specified by the employer (first aid or cardiopulmonary resuscitation (CPR) certification).

   You may wish to include additional items in an appendix, such as other permits or licenses that you think strengthen the case you are making about your ability to do the job, acknowledgments of participation in professional associations and conferences, and letters of appreciation for profession-related service.

4. *Professional Practice*: This section of the portfolio should include carefully selected artifacts that demonstrate your knowledge, skills, and dispositions appropriate to the type of employment you are seeking. Table 7.12 provides a sample job description with examples in the adjacent column of artifacts you might use to demonstrate one's competence.

Portfolios used for Promotion

Portfolios have become widely accepted as tools to assess students' development and learning at all levels—from infancy through graduate school. The value of this practice has not been lost on administrators where employee development and competency are concerned. Increasingly, assessment by portfolio is being adopted as a means to determine an employee's promotability in the employment setting. Guidelines for promotion portfolios vary widely. In some instances, employers are highly prescriptive—indicating in great detail the numbers, kinds, and levels of activities to be included. On the other end of the spectrum, promotion guidelines can be quite general—asking the candidate

Table 7.12 Sample Job Description with Examples of Artifacts

Sample Job Description with Examples of Artifacts	
Sample Lead Preschool Teacher Job Description	**Location and Examples of Evidence in the Portfolio**
Responsibilities	
The care, safety, and well-being of all children in the group	Professional Background: Résumé. Detail your previous experience in which you were responsible for groups of children.
Planning and implementing developmentally appropriate curriculum for preschoolers	Professional Background: Philosophy statement. Professional Practice: A web of an integrated curriculum unit, an outline of a curriculum project, a summary of curriculum activities in a content area such as literacy, a lesson plan.
Setting up the physical environment to meet the changing needs and interests of the children and in accordance with health and safety requirements	Professional Background: Philosophy statement. Professional Practice: Photographs, with narratives, of environments you have managed and shaped.
Modeling best practice and ethical practice as defined by NAEYC	Professional Background: Philosophy statement. Professional Practice: Best practice can be addressed in the brief narratives that accompany curriculum, staff development, and parent involvement artifacts.
Participating in regular staff meetings and other professional development activities	Professional Background: Certificates of conference participation, awards, etc. Professional Practice: Summary of contributions you have made toward staff development in previous positions.
Maintaining positive relationships and regular communication with parents	Professional Background: Philosophy statement. Professional Practice: Parent newsletter.
Supervising assistants, parent volunteers, and other classroom personnel as required	Professional Background: Résumé noting supervision responsibilities Professional Practice: Photographs, with narratives, of parent involvement in the classroom.
Working as part of a team	Professional Background: Philosophy statement. Professional Practice: Flyer and photographs, with narratives, of center festival, fundraiser, parent night, staff training, letter of appreciation.

Table 7.12 *Continued*

Professional Background	
AA in child development or equivalent	Résumé
Courses/certification required to meet state requirements	Certificates, transcripts
2 years of full-time experience as a teacher or assistant teacher in early care and education	Résumé and letters of recommendation
Current certification in child CPR	Certificate
General knowledge of nutrition and first aid	Résumé
Good health as verified by a physician's statement	Health form or letter from physician on letterhead
Tuberculosis clearance	Certificate
Fingerprint clearance	Photocopy of fingerprint card or other acceptable form

to represent the experiences that they believe characterize their readiness for a new level of responsibility as they perceive it. Regardless of criteria, promotion portfolios can provide an excellent vehicle for reflection and goal setting.

In preparing a promotion portfolio, you might consider including the following topic areas:

- Philosophy of education,
- Pedagogical approach,
- Global reflection on professional growth,
- Curriculum vitae (all relevant experience and education),
- Accomplishments, and
- Evidence (personal documents and artifacts).

The four types of portfolios we have discussed—developmental, showcase, assessment, and professional—can all be adapted to suit almost any need that builders might have with regard to documenting their professional growth and development. Regardless of purpose or type, however, a portfolio will most likely be subject to one or more reviews.

Assessment: Formative and Summative Looks at Portfolios

Each of the portfolio types we have described—developmental, showcase, assessment, and professional—is designed to present an accurate point-in-time portrait of its builder. Each has its unique characteristics, and yet each holds characteristics in common. One of the things they hold in common is that all portfolios undergo some form of review or assessment. For purposes of this discussion, we first want to clarify a few terms associated with assessment.

The words *assessment* and *evaluation* are often used interchangeably in the literature to mean measuring or assigning comparative value in relation to criteria or in a ranking. Sometimes these words are differentiated. *Assessment* is used when describing progress toward a goal but without assigning value; *evaluation* is used to mean assigning value, as in the first definition.

We use the word *assessment* throughout this book, and we distinguish between two types: formative and summative. We define *formative assessment* as descriptive of an ongoing process of review and revision toward a goal of mastery. For instance, a student may submit a draft of his philosophy statement. The student and instructor may use a rubric to determine the clarity and completeness of the statement, and identify areas for clarification or revision. Kilbane and Milman (2003) illustrate formative assessment with this characterization:

> imagine a chef tasting a soup while she is cooking it. Because the soup is still in its formative stage, the chef can change the recipe as needed to improve the soup. If the chef's goal is to produce a tasty soup, then all evaluation evolves around investigating this characteristic—not texture or color of the soup. (p. 80)

We define *summative assessment* as assigning value and making a determination of quality against external criteria. It describes where a person is in relation to a specific set of skills, a knowledge base, or dispositions at a given time. It is a measure of whether, or the degree to which, a person has achieved proficiency. Outcomes, such as the awarding of a grade for an assignment or course, result from summative assessments. Kilbane and Milman (2003) illustrate summative assessment in this way:

> imagine a crowd at a dinner party tasting and deciding how well they like the soup the chef has made. At this point, it is too late for the chef to improve the soup. It is left up to the crowd to judge its quality. They each have ideas about what quality means. Each will decide how well the soup measures up to their idea of what soup would taste like, look like, and smell like. Then sometimes the crowd will make a judgment about how good the chef is based on her soup. (p. 80)

Portfolio builders, who are familiar with the assessment tools that will be applied to their portfolios, are in a position to make informed decisions regarding content and presentation. The type of assessment employed will depend on the purpose for which the portfolio was designed, or where it is in the process of being developed. For instance, a rubric might be used for formative assessment as the portfolio is being developed. Revisions will be aimed at bringing the quality of the portfolio to a higher level on the rubric. The same rubric might then be used for summative assessment. Grades or other decisions will be based on the finished product. In the following sections we discuss rubrics, checklists, and peer and instructor critiques. We have included examples of each of these tools.

Rubrics

Rubrics are frequently used as tools to assess a piece of work's level of quality. Rubrics present a continuum of scoring criteria with descriptions that identify the levels of quality. One advantage of using rubrics is that those who will be judged by them have the final assessment criteria to use as a guide while developing their portfolios. Another advantage of rubrics is that they provide the assessor with a tool that helps ensure a greater measure of consistency and standardization across multiple portfolios. Table 7.13 shows a scoring rubric for portfolios that we adapted from

Table 7.13 Portfolio Scoring Rubric

Content	Developing	Competent	Accomplished
Evidence (artifacts and personal documents)	Few artifacts and personal documents are related to one or more of the standards, and connections between evidence and criteria may be murky. Evidence of professional practice is sometimes unclear.	Most artifacts and personal documents are related to one or more of the standards, and connections are logical and clear. Evidence of professional practice is provided.	All artifacts and personal documents are clearly and directly related to one or more of the standards, and very clear connections are made between all evidence and criteria. Strong evidence of professional practice is provided.
Rationale	Lacks an accurate and/or complete description of evidence, reasons for selection of evidence are missing or trivial, connection to literature is inaccurate or missing, fails to demonstrate understanding of or competence in standard.	Description of evidence is accurate and complete, reasons for selection of evidence may be unclear or not well-stated, connection to literature may be weak, partially demonstrates understanding of and competence in standard.	Description of evidence is accurate and complete, includes compelling reasons for selection of evidence, shows strong connection to the professional literature, demonstrates understanding of and competence in standard.

Captions	Captions do not accurately convey the content of the artifact. Writer uses extraneous words and/or does not explain who, what, when, where, why.	Captions convey most of pertinent information (who, what, where, when, why) but may not be concise.	Captions convey precisely and concisely what is in the illustration or photo; answer who, what, when, where, why; contain no extraneous words.
Reflections	A few reflections indicate insights and make connections to impact of learning and meaning to future actions.	Most reflections show insight and connections to past and present learning and experience with meaning to future actions.	Highly insightful. Thoughtful connections among past and present learning/ experience. Delineates implications for future action. Shows evidence of projection and planning.
Organization	Organization is somewhat obscure. Navigation is challenging for the reader. Signage is inconsistent or in some cases not present. Content groupings are somewhat confusing.	Organization is unclear in places, requiring careful attention in order to navigate successfully. Signage is not always consistent or obvious. Content groupings are not always logical.	Organization facilitates ease of navigation and access to supplementary evidence. Signage (e.g., contents, links, tabs) is clear and accurate. Content groupings are logically arranged.
Design and Layout	Graphic elements are not always complementary, sometimes confusing or distracting from the message.	Graphic elements are mostly complementary, adding interest and enhancing the message.	Graphic elements are used judiciously; to enhance message and add a dynamic quality to the finished product.
Writing Mechanics	Use of standard English, yet frequent errors in spelling, grammar, and syntax make reading difficult.	Use of standard English, but writing has some errors in spelling, grammar, and syntax.	Excellent use of standard English with no errors in spelling, grammar, or syntax. Writing is fluid, clear, and coherent.

Source: Adapted from Montgomery & Wiley, *Creating E-Portfolios Using PowerPoint*, 2004.

Montgomery and Wiley (2004). We have organized ours using three levels: developing, competent, and accomplished. *Developing* indicates minimum, yet adequate proficiency. *Competent* reflects a level of accomplishment beyond the basics, indicating substantial grasp of content. *Accomplished* illustrates the highest level of synthesis and integration, effective communication, thoroughness, and a firm grasp of the complexities of teaching and learning.

We have included a second rubric, shown in Table 7.14, that is notable in two ways: (1) the criteria it measures are shown on the same page as the rubric; and (2) it has four levels of quality rather than the three in the Portfolio Scoring Rubric (Table 7.13). We use it with final student teachers in an early childhood credential program. The students are given the rubric at the beginning of the semester and are encouraged to use it as a guide while developing their course portfolio. It is later used by the supervisor in a summative assessment of the portfolio.

TABLE 7.14 Rubric for Final Student Teachers in Early Childhood Credential Program

EHD 160, Option II, final student teachers
Course assessment Portfolios:
Which are later adapted for Interview and *BTSA

Content Criteria
Reflection for each of the six domains/standards of the California Standards for the Teaching Profession.
Reflection can be written using the Past, Present, Future model.
At least 1 example of supporting evidence for each element for each standard.
Clear connections from evidence to elements.

Organization and Presentation Criteria
Six sections, one for each domain of the California Standards
Title/cover page, table of contents, tabs, neat, organized, typed, grammar/spelling

	Content	Organization and Presentation
Inadequate	Meets less than half the requirements	Looks careless and/or hurried, parts illegible. Multiple grammatical and stylistic or spelling errors.
Satisfactory	Each domain has a reflection and at least one piece of supporting evidence for each element	Content is typed but presentation appears rushed. Some errors in grammar and/or spelling but not interfere with clarity.
Strong	Insightful reflections for each domain, all artifacts clearly connected to elements	Clear, uncluttered and attractive. Easy to find specific information. Few grammatical and/or stylistic or spelling errors.
Outstanding	All domain reflections show growth and learning from experience, feedback and readings	Evidence that pride and care were taken and the message of product is clearly defined. Nearly error-free, reflecting clear understanding and thorough proofreading. Very user-friendly.

Checklists

Checklists provide guides for keeping track of the completion of required components and/or steps in the procedure. They are often used for self-pacing and sequencing of tasks; they are also used by mentors and instructors to monitor students' progress. This type of tool provides an organized way to keep track of what has been done and what remains to be done. The checklist in Table 7.15 can be helpful as you plan and develop your portfolio.

Most of the items on the checklist are covered in other parts of this book. We would add a special note about timelines, however. Keep in mind that portfolio development often ends up requiring much more time than you might anticipate. Include in your timeline the applicable items from the checklist. Be sure to plan in time to review the final document and make revisions or modifications as needed. If a due date is associated with the portfolio, you might find it helpful to begin with that date and work backward.

Peer and Instructor Feedback Critiques

It is the practice in many programs to provide opportunities for peer feedback on portfolios, in addition to that of instructors. These critiques can

Table 7.15 Checklist for Portfolio Development

Checklist for Portfolio Development
Check when the items have been completed

Stage 1. Preparation

___ Determine purpose, type, context and audience
___ Develop timeline
___ Decide on print or electronic format, or both
___ Develop a budget
___ Collect artifacts and personal documents that already exist
___ Develop artifacts and collect additional personal documents as needed
___ Select exemplars from body of evidence to include in portfolio

Stage 2. Building the portfolio

___ Title page
___ Table of contents (Categories for organizing content)
___ Self-introduction
___ Philosophy statement
___ Global reflection on professional growth
___ Project description (if applicable)
___ Reflections on subsections (as is appropriate)
      (individual standards or project)
___ Evidence (artifacts and personal documents) with explanation
      and connection to criteria

be used to provide assessment on parts of portfolios—partitive critiques—during the development phase of the work. They can also be used to assess the whole portfolio. In either case, the assessments can be either formative or summative.

When used to assess parts of portfolios, such as a teaching unit or a project, critiques are more narrowly focused on how the evidence meets a particular goal or standard/s within the criteria. When used to assess the whole portfolio, the focus is on how well the completed work conveys the message of competence in relation to the full criteria. Although peer or instructor critiquing may not be part of your setting, you can use this tool as a means of self-assessment. We have included a partitive critiquing form in Table 7.16.

Table 7.16 Portfolio Entry Critique

Portfolio Entry Critique		
Presenter		Critique by
Portfolio entry		Date
Standard/s addressed		
Criteria	**Rate 1–5 (1 = high)**	**Strengths and Suggestions for Improvement**
The intended audience/user of the activity or project is clear	1 2 3 4 5	
The purpose of the presentation or product is clear	1 2 3 4 5	
The evidence demonstrates strong connections to the identified standard/s	1 2 3 4 5	
The evidence clearly demonstrates competence (accomplishes the purpose)	1 2 3 4 5	
If supplementary evidence is used (e.g., items for inclusion in an appendix), it is consistent with the standard/s	1 2 3 4 5	
The content is well organized (follows logically with good connections throughout)	1 2 3 4 5	
The content is attractively and professionally presented	1 2 3 4 5	

A Final Note

Constructing a portfolio involves many challenges and opportunities. The ultimate challenge is to present unequivocal documentation that you know and can do what is specified in the criteria to which you are subject. This is no easy task. It requires diligence, perseverance, and focus. The challenges can seem formidable. And yet, there is much to be learned from taking them on. The opportunities and accomplishment lie in rising to the challenge. Portfolios offer the possibility for deep, personally meaningful learning that only comes about through a solid investment of time, energy, will, and commitment. Satisfaction is earned through a job well done.

eight

Structure, Design, and Construction of Print and Electronic Portfolios

Creative work is play. It is free speculation using materials of one's chosen form.

—Stephen Nachmanovitch

How many times have you picked up a book or magazine only to put it back down because it just did not appeal to you? Maybe the pages were too busy or the print was too crowded and small. Like books and magazines, portfolios are publications. The more appealing they are, the better chance they have of being read and taken seriously. This chapter is dedicated to helping you make choices necessary to creating a professional, finished product, whether in electronic or print form. We have included general guidelines that apply to both formats, followed by guidelines and suggestions specific to each format.

Print or Electronic Format?

Portfolios can be created in print or electronic format. In some cases, an instructor or program criteria will determine the format for you. In cases where you have a choice, you will need to consider a number of factors before deciding which format better suits your needs. Each format has its pluses and minuses, as you will see below.

Print Portfolios

Print portfolios are composed of materials that will be quite familiar to anyone who has been to school. They are most often housed in three-ring binders, although file boxes and accordion files are also used. Section dividers, tabs, good-quality paper, and page protectors are also typically used in print portfolios. These materials are relatively inexpensive and readily available.

The processes by which information is readied for inclusion in the portfolio will also be familiar. Artifacts and personal documents can be easily duplicated using a photocopier. We recommend that these items be duplicated in color where applicable, in order to preserve their original appearance. This would apply to items such as permits, certificates, and work samples. A cautionary note: Include copies of originals in your portfolio, rather than originals. Beyond the photocopier and word processor, support equipment is not necessary to create or view a print portfolio—no electricity or batteries required! Print portfolios are low-tech, requiring minimal technical skill on the part of the builder.

Print portfolios are stand-alone documents—what you see is what you get. This can be a plus or a minus. When the reader opens the portfolio, everything is there to see. No technical skill or know-how is required to move about and manipulate the pages. Because every item of support documentation is physically present, however, the portfolio can be bulky and unwieldy. If not organized well, then reading the portfolio often requires the reader to flip back and forth to view evidence associated with a particular topic. This physical manipulation can impair the sense of continuity and flow and become a distraction in and of itself. Other disadvantages with print portfolios include storage and duplication. Print portfolios are bulky to store. They are also costly, in both time and materials, to reproduce for distribution.

Electronic Portfolios

Electronic portfolios (e-portfolios) present opportunities and challenges to builders and readers alike. On the opportunity side, e-portfolios are compact, easy to store and distribute, and inexpensive to duplicate. The hyperlink feature common to e-portfolios makes navigating through them quite easy and efficient. It also facilitates a more flexible structure than is possible in print versions. Print versions necessarily follow a linear structure—one page follows another. Support documentation is often in an appendix at the back, adding to the document's bulk, complicating navigation, and compromising continuity. Electronic versions allow the reader to move about the document at will. Their nonlinear structure means that support documentation can be virtually attached where appropriate without compromising the overall continuity and flow of the document.

E-portfolios require access to technology, technical skill, and often a degree of technical support, which print versions do not. Readers must also have access to computer hardware and compatible software in order to read the portfolio. On the plus side, e-portfolios provide builders with an opportunity to display their technical competence—something that is now considered desirable or even essential in the contemporary teaching environment. Depending on the builder's knowledge of computers and familiarity with software applications, however, the learning curve can be quite steep, thus adding a measure of difficulty to the portfolio process.

Reproducing evidence for inclusion in an e-portfolio can be somewhat more complicated than doing it for print versions. Documents such as permits and work samples must be converted to digital images that are accessible electronically. Some of these technical issues are discussed in greater depth later in this chapter.

Once the choice has been made to "go electronic," a further decision must be made as to which type of e-portfolio to create. This decision may be dictated by the program in which you are enrolled. E-portfolios fall into two main categories. The first is web-based, created for display over the World Wide Web. The second category is non-web-based, created using presentation software.

Web-Based Portfolios

Web-based portfolios are designed to be viewed via the Internet. The builder creates a web page on which to display the portfolio, and that web page is posted to a server. Software, such as Microsoft Front Page or Adobe Dreamweaver, is used to design web pages. Because web-based portfolios are stored on servers rather than on the user's own computer, there may be costs associated with renting storage space on a server.

Web-based portfolios present several unique challenges. The first involves level of technical skill. Although computers, in many cases, have become part of everyday life, web-page design is still well outside of the experience or expertise of many users. Time must be invested, above and beyond that needed to build the portfolio, to acquire web-authoring skills. However, tools for creating web-based portfolios are becoming increasingly user-friendly, accessible, and interactive with the advent of Web 2.0. The second challenge has to do with accessibility. Web-based portfolios are potentially accessible by anyone anywhere in the world who has access to the Internet. Although Internet security is improving, it still must be considered, as portfolios often contain personal and contact information. Additionally, with web-based portfolios the intended readers of the portfolios must have Internet access, some degree of technical know-how in order to view them, and often passwords.

Non-Web-Based Portfolios

Non-web-based portfolios are usually created using presentation software. Once produced, they are saved to a CD, DVD, flash drive, or memory card. This makes them very portable, easy to distribute and store, and secure. The Internet is not a factor in this type of portfolio. The builder controls distribution by providing the intended audience with a CD, DVD, flash drive, or memory card. These e-portfolios can also be uploaded onto the Web for viewing by an intended audience.

The simplest type of electronic portfolio is that used for developmental purposes. Developmental portfolios, as we use them, are often comprised of a set of electronic files and subfiles that are shared between the builder and the instructor or mentor. They are not configured on presentation software. All other portfolio types—showcase, assessment, and professional—require a more complex organizational structure. This structure is facilitated by presentation software.

PowerPoint is presentation software that is readily adapted to portfolio work. It is a software application within Microsoft Office, an integrated software package that includes, at a minimum, word processing (Word) and spreadsheet (Excel) applications. The integrated nature of this software facilitates easy transfer of documents that have been created in one application (e.g., Word) to other applications in the same package (e.g., PowerPoint).

We prefer using PowerPoint with students, rather than web-based tools or other presentation software, for several reasons. First, most students have some familiarity with it and ready access to it. Second, because it is easy to learn and use, the amount of time a student spends to become reasonably proficient is minimal. This applies to those who are new to computers and also to those who have never used presentation software. Third, PowerPoint gives users a lot of flexibility and a range of tools for individualizing their documents. And fourth, because this software is so widely used, readers of portfolios are likely to have it available for viewing the documents.

Structuring Portfolios

We have provided three outlines, shown in Table 8.1, to guide you in structuring your portfolio of choice: one for showcase portfolios, one for assessment portfolios, and one for professional portfolios used for job interviews. The outlines list the basic features that readers in various contexts might expect to find. You may decide to include others, and, of course, the criteria for your particular portfolio will act as a guide to your inclusions.

Table 8.1 Outlines for Showcase, Assessment, and Professional Portfolios

Showcase Portfolios	Assessment Portfolios	Professional (Interview) Portfolios
Title slide or page	Title slide or page	Title slide or page
Table of contents Navigation map (used in electronic showcase or other portfolios in which clusters of standards are addressed in the same entry)	Table of contents	Table of contents
Self-introduction	Self-introduction	May include a letter of introduction
Philosophy statement Global reflection on growth	Philosophy statement Global reflection	Philosophy statement Professional growth plan
Project description—a slide or page for each project that includes a brief description of the project and each standard addressed in the project		
Major learning achieved— slides or pages for each project that relay learning associated with each standard the project addresses	Major learning achieved— slides or pages for each standard that relay learning associated with respective standard addressed	
Evidence slides or pages— includes artifacts and personal documents, rationales, references to the standard/s or requirement/s, reflections associated with specific standards or projects	Evidence slides or pages—includes artifacts and personal documents, rationales, references to the standard/s or requirement/s, reflections associated with specific standards or projects	Documentation of professional practice, transcripts, résumé, permits,licenses, certificates, and clearances (e.g., TB, health) indicated in the job description, letters of recommendation, awards and certificates related to professional development and service Any other documentation requested by the employer can usually be integrated into the above categories

Portfolio Features for Print or Electronic Portfolios

Showcase, assessment, and professional portfolios hold some features in common, such as title pages/slides and statements of philosophy, whereas some features are unique to a particular portfolio type (shown in Table 8.1).

The features we have included here are common to both print and electronic portfolios. Where the features of portfolio types are held in common, we have provided a single example below that can be applied to all. In the cases where features differ from one type to another, we have included samples for each portfolio type that address their uniqueness. You will notice that, in the examples, our sample e-portfolio slides are shown in landscape orientation, rather than in portrait view. This is because Power-Point defaults to landscape view in its layout of slides. Portrait view must be selected, but is not well suited to the portfolio application. The type and quantity of information you wish to display is better suited to some slide layouts than to others. Experiment with various layouts to determine which work best. We have used a variety of slide layouts in the e-portfolio examples that accompany the discussion of the features below. These examples will give you an idea of the possibilities available in PowerPoint.

Regardless of portfolio type, we remind you that the examples we have provided are just that—examples. Use them as a guide, but do not let them limit your imagination and creativity.

Title Page

Every portfolio, print or electronic, needs a title page/slide. The visual appeal of the title page/slide is important (Figure 8.1), because it provides an opportunity to make a good first impression and provides the reader with information that identifies the builder. This would include your name and the title of your portfolio. It may also include the name of the program to which the portfolio is associated, the year in which the portfolio was completed, and any other information required in your instructions. As

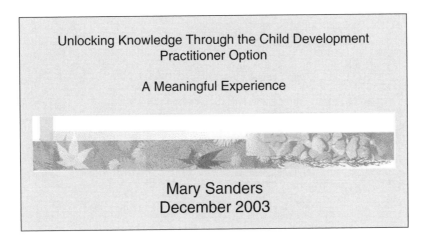

FIGURE 8.1 Title Slide

with every page/slide in your portfolio, you can configure it to best show the information and deliver your message. Print portfolios are often contained in binders. Presentation binders (those with transparent pockets on the outside front cover) work especially well, since the page inserted in the pocket can serve as both the portfolio cover and title page.

Table of Contents

Like the title page/slide, every portfolio type requires a table of contents. The table of contents will be different for each portfolio type, reflecting its unique features, organization, and entries. In each case, the table of contents has two main purposes. First, it informs the reader about what you have included in the document. Second, it tells the reader how you have organized the contents. Print portfolios use tabs and/or page numbers to indicate location of materials; e-portfolios use hyperlinks in lieu of page numbers for navigation purposes. Links will be covered later in this chapter. We have included three variations on the e-portfolio table of contents. Figure 8.2 is from a professional portfolio. Figures 8.3 and 8.4 are both from showcase portfolios. Figures 8.2 and 8.3 are linear versions—that is, they are organized in an outline form, such as one you might find in a book. This format suggests movement through the document in a straight line. Figure 8.4 is in a nonlinear form. It is organized as a diagram or web, which invites moving about on the basis of interest.

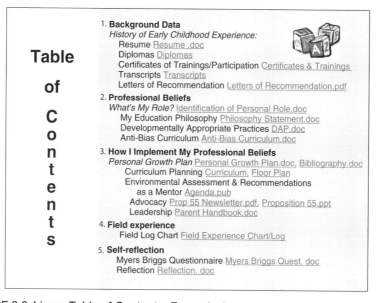

FIGURE 8.2 Linear Table of Contents, Example 1

Table of Contents

Self Introduction Mainline slide with link to full documents.doc

Philosophy Statement Philosophy statement.ppt

Reflection on Professional Growth Reflection on professional growth.ppt

Project 1: <u>Name of project here</u> Project description showcase port.ppt

Standards met Standards met.ppt

Major Learning Achieved Major learning achieved.ppt

Evidence (with links) Evidence slide with link.ppt

(Note: This Project format will be repeated for each project)

FIGURE 8.3 Linear Table of Contents, Example 2

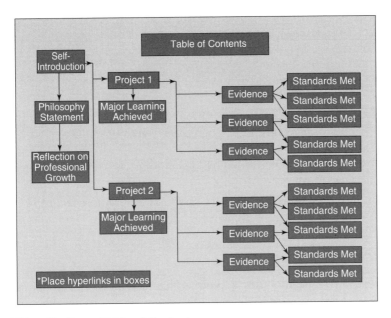

FIGURE 8.4 Nonlinear Table of Contents

Self-Introduction

The self-introduction is another page/slide that may be included in print or electronic portfolios. Shown in Figure 8.5, it offers readers a glimpse into who you are and gives them a chance to get to know you. Different portfolio builders approach the content of this in various ways. Some give it a personal slant; some give it a more professional slant. There is no "right way." You might provide a personal story about how and why you entered the early care and education field, or relay something of your professional goals. You might choose to talk about the intersection of your personal and professional lives. These and other approaches can be very effective.

Self-Introduction

I first worked with children in the Future Teachers of America (FTA) Club in high school. I was introduced to the joys of helping children and witnessing their growth. I had a part in helping them succeed and knew I wanted to be a part of that. I chose a career in Child Development, working during the day and going to school at night. In 1991, I graduated with an Associate's degree in Child Development and began teaching in an early childhood program.

I love touching the lives of children. Now, through the Child Development Practitioner Option program I have earned my BS degree. I've had the opportunity to learn more about the ECE field and further my education so that I can better serve children and families. I am an ECE professional.

FIGURE 8.5 Self-Introduction

The approach you take should be guided by two things:

1. The purpose for which you are developing the portfolio—keep your audience in mind.
2. The type of content that you are most comfortable revealing—let your comfort level be your guide.

Philosophy Statement

Every portfolio type includes a philosophy statement. In an e-portfolio, space on a slide is limited. Therefore, depending on its length, you may choose to summarize it on this slide and include a link to the entire document. The slide layout shown in Figures 8.6 and 8.7 is useful for documents, such as a philosophy statement, where text is the primary means of delivering information, as opposed to photographs or other graphics.

Reflection on Overall Professional Growth

Reflection is the defining characteristic of all portfolios. This type of reflection statement, as shown in Figure 8.8, is intended to provide an overview of your growth and change through your experiences as a student as part of a class or program (for showcase and assessment portfolios), or throughout your career thus far (professional portfolios). You will also provide reflections throughout the portfolio in conjunction with, and as part of, your evidence.

A Summary

- The teacher acts as a guide and a resource in child-initiated activities, promoting a safe and nurturing environment.

- Each child is viewed as an individual with different needs and is encouraged to be self-directed.

- It is important that the classroom provide spacious learning centers with active learning experiences suitable for varying developmental stage and individual needs.

Click here for full document

FIGURE 8.6 Philosophy Statement Summary with Link

Philosophy Statement

I believe that schools are first and foremost places where children learn to get along in a social world. Learning, whether it's arithmetic or dodge ball, is based in social interchange. More than anyone, Vygotsky has influenced my thinking about learning.

As a teacher, my job is to help children become socially competent. Research has shown that children who know how to make friends and feel competent and secure are more likely to succeed acedemically than those who don't. Since every child is unique and has a different history from everyone else, my role is to create an environment where each child can thrive because all children are intrinsically motivated to learn.

The environment should be responsive to children's interests and their learning styles. I believe that there is not just one way to learn a thing. The environment should also take in more than the classroom. The children's families and neighborhoods provide good sources of curriculum that extend the classroom.

FIGURE 8.7 Philosophy Statement

Project Description

Figure 8.9 conveys information about a specific project within a showcase portfolio. It contains a brief description of the project and identifies the standards that have been met through the project. Each project in the port-folio will have a project description.

Reflections
on Professional Growth

❖ I have moved from seeing myself as a teacher who has a job, to an early childhood educator who has a profession. I have recently taught a seminar on literacy for a *CCAEYC* conference. Before the Practitioner program I would have never seen myself as qualified to teach other teachers. I have also gained knowledge and self-confidence as a teacher of young children.

FIGURE 8.8 Reflection on Overall Professional Growth

Project 1: Assessing Desired Results

Project Description

This project focused on improving my management of the documentation process required for the California Department of Education Desired Results (DR). I felt that my observation process was fragmented and unintentional. Although the curriculum I provide develops the skills children need to meet DR, I did not effectively manage the documenting of those skills.

In this project, I set out answer the question: How do I make lesson plans, the curriculum goals, and the daily assessment process manageable to accomplish systematic documentation of Desired Results?

Standards met in this project:
Standard 3 – Observing, documenting & assessing...
Standard 4d – Building meaningful curriculum

FIGURE 8.9 Project Description

Major Learning Achieved

Showcase and assessment portfolios contain slides addressing major learning achieved. In the case of a showcase portfolio, the content focuses on the learning achieved in relation to a particular project. In assessment portfolios, it focuses on the learning achieved through the conduct of various types of activities. In both cases, concentrate on the big ideas you came away with. You should present the details of your learning—what you know and can do—in the evidence section that follows (Figure 8.10).

Evidence

Substantive evidence validates your claims of competence. Every portfolio type includes evidence: personal documents and artifacts. Your rationales and captions tell the reader what they are looking at, how and why you used it, with whom you used it, what you hoped to achieve through its use, and what it means in relation to the criteria it documents. It often takes more than one page/slide to present evidence. At the same time, however, it is important to be mindful of the total number of pages/slides you use. Keep this number manageable for the reader. In e-portfolios, use hyperlinks to

Major Learning Achieved

☐ All children's culture and language need to be represented in the classroom.

☐ These differences are important and need to be promoted to increase the understanding of differences. When this is done children feel comfortable and welcomed. If one culture is primarily represented, children from a different culture may feel they need to be more like that culture to be of value. This breaks down their self worth.

☐ Learning about the cultures and languages of the children aids in accurate assessments of them (e.g., If a child is bilingual, his language may be delayed but may not be a developmental problem).

FIGURE 8.10 Culture and Language Emphasized

connect the reader to additional documentation that can provide more complete evidentiary support when necessary. In print portfolios, use an appendix for additional support documents.

Include graphics where appropriate. Let the reader see what you are talking about. A picture *can* be worth a thousand words if selected carefully. You might use photos of a group of children engaged in a project or lesson, photos of the workshop in which you delivered your presentation, children's work samples, or diagrams of your own design (Figure 8.11). Graphics make this part of the portfolio come alive.

Release for Photographs

Portfolio evidence frequently includes photographs of human subjects. As you prepare artifacts for inclusion in your portfolio, make sure that you have permission from, or for, those whose images you capture in photographs, video, or film. Note that, at many child care programs and school sites, blanket permission is obtained from parents that allow use of pictures of their children for educational or publicity purposes. It is important for you to:

- know the policies and procedures regarding photo release in the setting in which you work,

Play Workshop

This was a workshop for parents to learn about the benefits of play and how to encourage play at home. The goals of this workshop included:

- Helping parents understand the importance of play for children
- Helping parents identify the 5 developmental domains of children and the benefits of play for each domain
- Helping parents create enriching play experience at home for thier children
- Giving parents resources for age-appropriate activities that promote playful experiences.

This workshop was 1 hour long. It included an introduction, an overhead presentation, hands-on activities, parent resources, and a conclusion.

FIGURE 8.11 Evidence Slide with Link

- determine whether or not the policy covers your intended use,
- if needed, obtain permission from the proper authority (child care program, school site, or parent/guardian), and
- keep a copy of release forms for your records.

Figure 8.12 gives you an idea of what you might include in a form of your own design.

Design Tips

We have included some tips to guide you in constructing your portfolio. Let your eye, and these tips, be your guide when designing your pages/slides.

Kilbane and Milman (2003) identify four principles of graphic design: contrast, repetition, alignment, and proximity. We have included a fifth principle: use of graphic elements. These principles work together to create a sense of balance, congruence, and professionalism in the finished product. They can also work against each other, creating products that confuse the eye or distract the reader.

Contrast refers to the degree of difference between graphic elements. Graphic elements consist of any item used on a page/slide (e.g., background color of the page or slide, text, pictures, colors, the sizes of objects, or the sizes or styles of fonts). An example of contrast is black print on white paper. The sharp contrast makes reading the text very easy. One of the most common errors made in e-portfolios is when the background color of

---

Photograph Release

I grant permission to _____ to use my photograph and/or the photograph of my child, in publications developed and used for educational purposes. By signing this permission form, I am agreeing that there will be no compensation to me or my child for use of these materials.

I release _____ from liability that might stem from the inclusion of these materials in educational publications.

Name_____Child's name_____
        Print Name Clearly   Print Name Clearly

Signature_____

Address_____

FIGURE 8.12 Sample Photo Release

the slide and the color of the text are too similar (e.g., tan background with yellow text).

Repetition is another important principle. Repeating elements through-out your document helps create a sense of continuity and order. A consis-tent color scheme, background, and font and/or graphics that are similar in design help to unify the portfolio and keep it from looking like a patchwork of disconnected pages.

Alignment is the third principle to consider. This principle addresses the placement of elements on your pages/slides. The eye looks for symmetry or balance. Even asymmetrical configurations can convey a sense of balance. Alignment requires consideration of the whole space—edge to edge. Margins, blank space, and graphic elements must work together. In e-portfolios, pay special attention to margins and text/graphics box edges. PowerPoint does not recognize the edges of a slide in the way that a word-processing program recognizes the margins of a page. In PowerPoint, the boxes in which you posi-tion text and graphics will run off the edges of the slide, sending your text into parts unknown if you overfill them or insert unnecessary page returns.

Proximity relates to how close graphic elements are to one another. Elements that are related to one another go together. Elements that are dis-similar should enjoy a separation. As Kilbane and Millman (2003) point out, "This grouping contributes to the organization of information for both the eye and the mind" (p. 139).

Use of graphic elements is of concern when designing a portfolio. Portfolio builders sometimes have a tendency to include too many graphic elements. While these can dress up a document and add interest, too much embel-lishment to background, font styles, word art, borders, stickers, or other elements can overwhelm your message. Use them with care. Also remember that hyperlinks and action buttons are graphic elements. It is good practice to place them in the same position on each slide, for example, the lower right-hand corner. Another caution: Be careful when using borders or back-grounds with bold designs or strong colors over which you have placed text because overlaying backgrounds or borders with text can diminish or obscure the text—thus losing effectiveness. Make sure the text can be easily seen and read.

Special Design Tips for PowerPoint Users

These tips are included to ease the transition to PowerPoint for those who may be unfamiliar with the program. They include a brief explanation of how PowerPoint treats font, the use of automation and sound effects, and the use of auto-play.

Font and font size defaults (automatic settings) on PowerPoint are set so that the text can be read from across a room. The default font is Arial; the default font size depends on the type of text box used. Title boxes default to 40-point font, subtitle boxes default to 32-point font, and text boxes default to 28-point font. In general, these size fonts are too large for use on portfolio slides. A font size of 16–18 points works well for body text in many fonts. Keep readability in mind when making your selections. Choose two or three fonts at the most, and use them consistently throughout your portfolio. The same goes for font sizes. Limit them to two or three. These limitations will help you avoid visual clutter.

Animation and sound effects available on PowerPoint are great fun. You can usually spot a document created by a new user because everything that jumps and sputters is included. Have fun experimenting with them, but use these features in your final document sparingly on individual pages and throughout the document. They should enhance your message and add interest, rather than detract from what you are trying to get across. Remember that they can also frustrate the reader who is made to wait while graphics dance and fly.

In determining whether or not to use *auto-play*, ask yourself if it adds to or detracts from your message, and whether or not it is helpful to your readers. Because portfolios are "user-run or interactive presentations" (Weverka, 2010), auto-play is not generally recommended for portfolios. However, if you use auto-play, allow enough time on each slide for the reader to read the content. Check this by having someone who is unfamiliar with the content read it through for you, rather than timing it yourself. Your intimate knowledge of the content will enable you to read it faster than someone who is seeing it for the first time.

Using PowerPoint to Create an Electronic Portfolio

The idea of e-portfolios is new to many adults with whom we work. Some find the prospect exciting and challenging. Others approach it with trepidation or even fear. We have found that a few notes of explanation, some organizational guidance, and some design pointers are usually enough to get builders moving in the right direction. We have included all of these in the next sections.

Notes of Explanation

This is not meant to be a complete guide to using PowerPoint. Rather, we provide a brief introduction to the application terminology that you will encounter and to the features that we consider indispensable to portfolio development.

PowerPoint is primarily intended for use in developing presentations that will be projected onto a large screen for viewing by a group. Portfolio development is an adapted use. Portfolio viewing is usually done up close on a personal computer screen by a single individual or small group. This difference has implications for how slides are designed, for the amount of content displayed on a slide, and for font size (see the discussion on design tips above). Portfolios have an interactive aspect that is facilitated by hyperlinks with which the reader can navigate the portfolio.

If you are new to PowerPoint, some of its terminology may be unfamiliar to you. PowerPoint uses *slide* instead of *page* to indicate where, and on what, the document content is depicted. We use the term *slide* when referring to pages in an e-portfolio.

Layout is another term with which you need to be familiar. A slide layout includes boxes for text and boxes for objects, such as clip art, photographs, and charts. The slide layout controls placement of your content. PowerPoint provides a number of preprogrammed layouts from which to choose. These layouts can be changed and rearranged to suit your design purpose. PowerPoint also gives you the flexibility to construct your own layouts using blank slides. Figure 8.13 is an example of a layout. It includes a box for the heading, a box for text, and a box for an object, in this case, clipart.

Another PowerPoint term that will be useful is *design template*. Like slide layouts, design templates are preprogrammed configurations that incorporate backgrounds and color schemes that you can choose to apply to individual slides or whole documents. Backgrounds range from solid colors to those that appear textured. They can also include graphics, from simple borders to full-slide pictorial images. These features, when used judiciously,

Child in Crisis: A case study of Joey
Evidence for Standards 1, 2, and 3

- Action research project focused on Joey, a child in crisis.

- Used knowledge of child development, library research, systematic observation, & collegial collaboration to assess Joey

- Developed, documented & assessed intervention in the classroom

- Involved parents and community professionals.

- Identified community resources.

- And sparked a desire to further research Dr. B. D. Perry's work on "The Vortex of Violence." (1996)

FIGURE 8.13 Layout and Background, Example 1

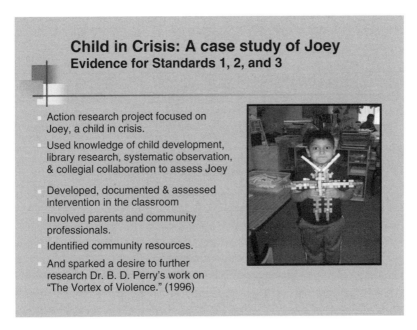

Child in Crisis: A case study of Joey
Evidence for Standards 1, 2, and 3

- Action research project focused on Joey, a child in crisis.
- Used knowledge of child development, library research, systematic observation, & collegial collaboration to assess Joey
- Developed, documented & assessed intervention in the classroom
- Involved parents and community professionals.
- Identified community resources.
- And sparked a desire to further research Dr. B. D. Perry's work on "The Vortex of Violence." (1996)

FIGURE 8.14 Layout and Background, Example 2

lend continuity and interest to a portfolio. Figure 8.14 is the same slide as Figure 8.13 using a design template. If you find a background that you like, but it is too dark, you may be able to lighten it by clicking on *Design*, then on *Background Styles*, then on *Format Background*. Slide the *Transparency* controller to the desired percentage.

E-portfolios are developed on two levels. We call the first level the *mainline*. Mainline slides (Figure 8.15) are those that are visually present in the main body of the portfolio. Many mainline slides contain *hyperlinks*. Hyperlinks, also called links, connect the reader to slides anywhere within the mainline. Links that enable navigation within the mainline allow the reader to skip around the portfolio. The table of contents may contain links to each section of the portfolio. Hyperlinks embedded in the table of contents make the reader's job easier by providing maximum flexibility and navigability.

The hyperlink feature also enables navigation between the mainline slides and support evidence stored in files outside of the PowerPoint structure. This use of hyperlinking allows the portfolio builder to create the equivalent of an appendix. We call this second level of the portfolio *linked documents*. The hyperlink embedded in text looks like this: *Math Lesson*. It contains a word or phrase associated with the document. The feature gives readers the option of going deeper into your work as their needs or interests dictate.

Hyperlinking is such an important feature in the development of e-portfolios that we have included instructions on how to do it. Links have two forms

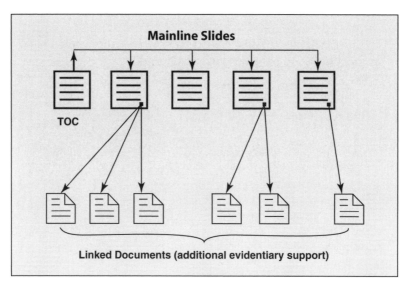

FIGURE 8.15 Mainline Hyperlinked to Support Documents

in PowerPoint. The first is a word or phrase inserted into the text where the hyperlink is needed. The second is an action button. It is important to note that action buttons are intended to be used in slide-show mode. They only work when the presentation is actually being shown, hence the word *action*. On a PowerPoint slide, the two forms look like those in the examples in Figure 8.16.

Because portfolios are often burned to CDs or DVDs, or saved on flash drives, we recommend the following steps as a matter of course when inserting hyperlinks (Figure 8.17). Cox and Lambert (2010) provide this tip: "PowerPoint 2010 does not support the direct burning of content to a DVD. If you prefer to burn to a DVD rather than a CD, first use the Package for CD feature to create a presentation package in a folder on your computer, and then use DVD-burning software to copy the package to the DVD" (p. 340).

The hyperlink embedded in text looks like this: Math Lesson. It contains a word or phrase associated with the document

The hyperlink in the form of an action button can be scaled to size. It looks like this:

FIGURE 8.16 Types of links: Underlined or Icon

Step 1: Preparation for hyperlinking documents

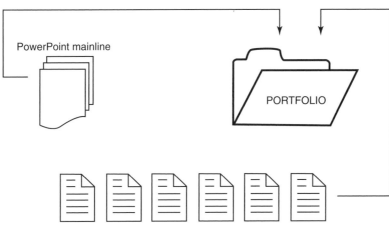

FIGURE 8.17 **Preparing for Hyperlinking Documents**

Step 1: Create a Master File

Create a file into which you save your PowerPoint mainline slides and all of the other files or documents to which you will create links. This step helps you avoid problems later when your link goes looking for files to open and cannot find them because they are scattered all over your hard drive. After you have completed Step 1, you can begin inserting hyperlinks (Step 2a or 2b).

Step 2a: Create Hyperlinks in PowerPoint Slides

Open your PowerPoint mainline. Select the slide onto which the hyperlink will be placed. Place the cursor where you want the hyperlink on a particular slide. Type in the descriptor for the document to which you will link (e.g., Parent Handbook, Lesson Plan) and highlight it. Go to *Insert* on the toolbar, scroll down to *Hyperlink* and click. The descriptor you typed will appear in the *Text to Display* box. Use the *Browse* box to find your document, and double click on it. The descriptor you highlighted on your slide will become the link and will look like this *Parent Handbook*. If you choose to insert action buttons instead of hyperlinks in text, as shown in Figure 8.16, follow the steps in 2b.

Step 2b: Create Hyperlinks Using Action Buttons

Type a word or phrase onto your slide. Go to *Slide Show* on the toolbar, scroll to *Action Buttons* and select the button of choice. Place the crosshairs next to your word or phrase, hold down the left click side of the mouse, drag the cursor to size the button, and release.

In the *Action Settings* box, select *Hyperlink To* and scroll down to the appropriate choice. If you are linking to another slide within your mainline, select from the scroll menu for choices such as *first slide*, *previous slide*, or *next slide*. If you are linking to a document outside of the PowerPoint presentation, select *Other File*. Locate the file you want using the *Hyperlink to Other File* box. Select the file. The link is complete. It will

look like this: 📄 Click here for Lesson Plan. Complete the linking process
Action button

between all desired mainline slides and support documents in your portfolio.

Step 3: Create a Copy of Your Portfolio for Distribution

The moral of the story here is that, if you have taken care to create the master file as directed above, you can then burn the entire master file (PowerPoint mainline slides and all linked documents) to a CD, DVD, or save on a flash drive *and keep your links intact!*

Converting Documents for Inclusion in the Portfolio

Scanning is one of the ways that print documents are converted to digital form. Scanning allows you to capture and save these items as digital files that can then be imported to the portfolio. Digital cameras also produce images that are easily uploaded to the electronic portfolio. Hard copies of original documents, such as transcripts, letters of recommendation, photographs, and permits, will have to be converted and saved in order for you to include them in your e-portfolio.

Word-processed documents that are free of graphics can be saved as Word documents, and can be imported directly to PowerPoint. Documents bearing graphic images, such as photographs and permits, will need to be saved as JPEG files, since this is the format most readily recognized by PowerPoint. If you do not have access to a scanner, scanning services are available at many commercial outlets that provide business services. Photographs taken with digital cameras are automatically saved as digital files to the camera's storage media (e.g., memory card, memory stick). They can be transferred directly from the storage device in the camera into PowerPoint as JPEG files. When converting documents, it is frequently necessary to crop or otherwise enhance them in order to achieve a professional-looking result. If you are not familiar with manipulating digital images, you may need to seek technical assistance.

Gentle Reminders

In this section, we present some suggestions related to writing conventions, organization, and tone that will enhance your portfolio's readability and appeal. While many of them may seem obvious, we have found that even the best writers benefit from an occasional reminder.

Writing Conventions

The portfolio represents you. As such, it is a tool that you can use to portray yourself as a competent communicator. All narrative statements, for example, the philosophy statement, explanations of artifacts, and reflections, should be well constructed, using standard English. You should write narratives in complete sentences with no errors in spelling, punctuation, grammar, or syntax. The exception to this is captions, which can be incomplete sentences but must be clear and descriptive. It is always a good idea to have someone proofread your documents. A fresh pair of eyes can pick up mistakes that you may have overlooked.

Organization

Make sure everything in the portfolio hangs together. Each entry's purpose and focus should be obvious. The reader should be able to follow your logic without difficulty and without asking questions such as, "Where did *that* come from?" or "What is this *connected* to?" A table of contents is a useful and necessary navigation tool and should be included regardless of portfolio type or format.

Tone

The tone you set in your portfolio will make an impression on the reader. Project a positive image. Look closely not only at what you say, but also how you say it. For instance, you might say, "I believe all children are capable of learning. A teacher's role is to individualize instruction so that every child works at his appropriate level." By contrast, a less positive way of saying this is, "I believe all children are capable of learning, but some will not be able to work at grade level because of their problems."

Tone also includes the use of person. Person reflects the degree of formality or familiarity used in your narrative. For example, when writing in the first person, the writer uses "I," as in "I believe . . ." It is appropriate in a portfolio to use the first person. After all, the portfolio is about you and what you can do.

Jargon is also an aspect of tone. Even though fellow educators are likely to be the readers of your portfolio, a good rule of thumb is to write as though the reader is unfamiliar with field-specific language, such as "zone of proximal development." Field-specific language includes acronyms. Even if you are sure the audience is familiar with the acronyms you use, always spell them out the first time they appear in your document. An example of an acronym often used in early care and education is DAP (developmentally appropriate practice).

A Final Note

Through the comparison of print and e-portfolios in this chapter, we have pointed out how similar they are in content and design, and yet how different they are in how they are constructed. Whether you choose to begin with a print or electronic portfolio, do keep in mind that once you have developed your portfolio in one format, you can quite easily develop a copy in the other format. Many of our teacher candidates, for instance, develop a print version and also an e-portfolio version that they can leave with prospective employers. Circumstances you encounter may suggest the need for both formats. Whichever format you use, your goal should be to display high-quality content in a medium that communicates it effectively. Keep this mantra in mind: Quality content and communication! Show your stuff.

References

Arnett, J. J. (2004). *Adolescence and emerging adulthood* (3rd ed.). Upper Saddle River, NJ: Prentice Hall.

Badrova, E., & Leong, D. J. (1996). *Tools of the mind: The Vygotskian approach to early childhood education.* Columbus, OH: Prentice Hall.

Bartell, C., Kaye, C., & Morin, J. (1998, Winter). Portfolio conversation: A mentored journey. *Teacher Education Quarterly, 132.*

Brookfield, S. D. (1986). *Understanding and facilitating adult learning: A comprehensive analysis of principles and effective practice.* San Francisco: Jossey-Bass.

Brookfield, S. D. (1987). *Developing critical thinkers: Challenging adults to explore alternative ways of thinking and acting.* San Francisco: Jossey-Bass.

Brookfield, S. D. (1995). *Becoming a critically reflective teacher.* San Francisco: Jossey-Bass.

Brookfield, S. D. (1996). Teacher roles and teaching styles. In A. C. Tuijnman (Ed.), *International encyclopedia of adult education and training* (2nd ed., pp. 529–534). Oxford: Elsevier Science.

Brown, J. D., & Wolfe-Quintero, K. (1997). Teacher portfolios for evaluation: A great idea or a waste of time? Retrieved from http://www.jaltpublications.org/tlt/files/97/jan/portfolios.html (accessed September 24, 2001).

Bullard, J. (2003). Constructivism: Does your practice match your conceptual framework? *Journal of Early Childhood Teacher Education, 24*(3). 157–162.

Burk, D. I., & Dunn, M. (1996, Summer). Learning about learning: An interactive model. *Action in Teacher Education, 18*(2). 11–18.

California Department of Education. (2010). *Early childhood educator competencies.* Sacramento.

Campbell, D. M., Cignetti, P. B., Melenyzer, B. J., Nettles, D. H., & Wyman, Jr., R. M. (2004). *How to develop a professional portfolio: A manual for teachers* (3rd ed.). Boston: Pearson.

Candy, P. C. (1991). *Self-direction for lifelong learning.* San Francisco: Jossey-Bass.

Cerbin, W. (1994). The course portfolio as a tool for continuous improvement of teaching and learning. *Journal on Excellence in College Teaching, 5*(1). 95–105.

Cox, J., & Lambert, J. (2010). *Microsoft PowerPoint 2010: Step by step*. Redmond, WA: Microsoft Press.

Cross, W. (1985). Black identity: Rediscovering the distinction between personal identity and reference group orientation. In M. B. Spencer, G. K. Brooklin, & W. R. Allen (Eds.). *Beginnings: The social and affective development of black children* (pp. 155–172). Hillside, NJ: Lawrence Erlbaum.

Curtis, D., & Carter, M. (2000). *The art of awareness: How observation can transform your teaching*. St. Paul, MN: Redleaf Press.

Daloz, L. A. (1999). *Mentor: Guiding the journey of adult learners*. San Francisco: Jossey-Bass.

Derman-Sparks, L. & Olsen Edwards, J. (2010). *Anti-bias education for young children and ourselves*. Washington, DC: National Association for the Education of Young Children.

DeVries, R., & Kohlberg, L. (1990). *Constructivist early education: Overview and comparison with other programs*. Washington, DC: National Association for the Education of Young Children.

Dewey, J. (1933). *How we think*. Boston: D. C. Heath and Company.

Dietz, M.E. (1995, Spring). Using portfolios as a framework for professional development. *Journal of Staff Development, 16*(2). 40–43.

Dunn, K. (October 2, 2000). Information literacy fact sheet. California State University. Retrieved from http://library.csun.edu/susan.curzon/fact_sheet.html (accessed August 9, 2010).

Erikson, E. (1963). *Childhood and society* (2nd ed.). New York: Norton.

Fink, L. D. (2003). Creating significant learning experiences: An integrated approach to designing college courses. San Francisco: Jossey-Bass.

Fosnot, C. (1996). Constructivism: A psychological theory of learning. In C. T. Fosnot (Ed.). *Constructivism: Theory, perspectives, and practice* (pp. 8–33). New York: Teachers College Press.

Froebel, F. (1826). *The education of man*. (W. N. Hailmann, Trans.). London: Appleton.

Frost, J. L., Wortham, S. C., & Reifel, S. (2005). *Play and child development*. Upper Saddle River, NJ: Pearson.

Gardner, H. (1983). *Frames of mind: The theory of multiple intelligences*. New York: Basic Books.

Goleman, D. (1995). *Emotional intelligence: Why it can matter more than IQ*. New York: Bantam Books.

Grant, G., & Huebner, T. (1998, Winter). The portfolio question: A powerful synthesis of the personal and professional. *Teacher Education Quarterly, 25*(1). 33–42.

Griffith, E. (April 27, 2010) Beginner's guide to PC backup. *PC Magazine*. Retrieved from http://www.pcmag.com/article2/0,2817,2363060,00.asp (August 22, 2010).

Harriman, P. L. (1941). Mental growth in children. In C. E. Skinner & P. L. Harriman, (Eds.). *Child psychology* (pp. 180–197). New York: The Macmillan Company.

Hawkins, C. & Black, S. (2004). Developing electronic portfolios across the State of Utah:

Breaks, breakdowns and breakthroughs. Retrieved from http://ww.haworthpress.com/web/CITS. Digital Object Identifier: 10.1300/Jo25v21n01-08

Hillocks, George, Jr. (1999). *Way of thinking, ways of knowing*. New York: Teachers College Press.

Hutchings, P., & Wutzdorff, A. (Eds.). (1988, Fall). *Knowing and doing: Learning through experience*. New Directions for Teaching and Learning, 35. San Francisco: Jossey-Bass.

Hyson, M. (Ed.). (2003). *Preparing early childhood professionals: NAEYC's standards for programs*. Washington, DC: National Association for the Education of Young Children.

Katz, L. (1995). *Talks with teachers of young children: A collection*. Norwood, NJ: Ablex Publishing.

Kilbane, C. R., & Milman, N. B. (2003). *The digital teaching portfolio handbook: A how-to guide for educators*. Boston: Allyn and Bacon.

Langer, E. J. (1997). *The power of mindful learning*. Cambridge: Perseus Publishing.

Lyons, N. (Ed.). (1998). *With portfolio in hand: Validating the new teacher professionalism*. New York: Teachers College Press.

McMillan, J. H. (2004). *Classroom assessment: Principles and practice for effective instruction* (3rd ed.). Boston: Pearson.

Mezirow, J. (1990). *Fostering critical reflection in adulthood*. Oxford: Jossey-Bass.

Mezirow, J. (1991). *Transformative dimensions of adult learning*. San Francisco: Jossey-Bass.

Mezirow, J. (2000). *Learning as transformation: Critical perspectives on a theory in progress*. San Francisco: Jossey-Bass.

Montgomery, K., & Wiley, D. (2004). *Creating e-portfolios using PowerPoint*. Thousand Oaks, CA: Sage Publications.

Paulson, F. L., Paulson, P. R., & Meyer, C. A. (1991). What makes a portfolio a portfolio? *Educational Leadership*, 48(5). 60–63.

Piaget, J., & Inhelder, B. (1969). *The psychology of the child*. New York: Basic Books.

Posner, G. (2005). *Field experience: A guide to reflective teaching*. Boston: Pearson.

Schon, D. A. (1983). *The reflective practitioner*. New York: Basic Books.

Shedroff, N. (1994). Information interaction design: A unified field theory of design. Retrieved from http:/www.nathan.com/thoughts/unified/ (accessed June 14, 2010).

Sockett, H. (1993). *The moral base for teacher professionalism*. New York: Teachers College Press.

Strachey, J. (Ed. & Trans.). (1969). *An outline of psychoanalysis*. New York: W. W. Norton.

Wardle, F (1996). Proposal: An anti-bias and ecological model for multicultural education. *Childhood Education*, 72(3). 152–156.

Webb, L. D., Metha, A., & Jordan, K. F. (1992). *Foundations of American education*. New York: Macmillan.

Weverka, P. (2010). *PowerPoint 2010: All-in-one for dummies*. Hoboken, NJ: Wiley.

What is a rationale statement and why do we write them? Retrieved from http://coe.ufl.edu/Courses/ITS/SSE4312/rationalehelp.htm (accessed September 3, 2010).

Wilcox, B. (1996, November). Smart portfolios for teachers in training. *Journal of Adolescent & Adult Literacy*, 40(3). 172.

Wolf, K., & Dietz, M. (1998, Winter). Teaching portfolios: Purposes and possibilities. *Teacher Education Quarterly* 25(1). 9–22.

Wolf, K., Lichtenstein, G., & Stevenson, C. (1997, March). Portfolios in teacher evaluation. Paper presented at the Annual Meeting of the American Educational Research Association, Chicago (ED 409 378).

Index

Note: Page numbers in *italics* are for tables, those in **bold** are for figures.